ALL THE WRITE MOVES

Your Essential Guide to Creating Great Fiction

By R.A. Paterson

By R.A. Paterson

YOUR INDISPENSABLE GUIDE!

Do you dream of creating great stories? Do you want to see your name on a book cover? Do you want others to admire you for your creative talent? Do you want your stories to stand out?

If any or all of these are true! This is the book for you!

All the Write Moves: Your Essential Guide to Creating Great Fiction is a handbook for new and experienced writers which covers the core ideas behind telling stories and writing fiction. Whether you're writing fiction, screenplays, graphic novels, television series, web serials, or just stories to tell your grandchildren, the core elements of story never change- and this book covers them all.

In this book you'll find:

- How the three-act story structure is rooted in our very idea of what stories are.
- Ways to make your book engaging and exciting to readers.
- Ways to write conflict and non-conflict based stories that resonate with readers.
- Simple, practical ways to structure your stories.
- Techniques to let you develop a full story from plot, character, setting, themes, or even your target audience.
- Easy ways to make your target audience fall in love with your characters.
- How to write scenes and sequences that fit together organically.
- Special tricks that authors have been using to brainstorm and develop ideas for decades.

- And so much more!

From the foundations of what a story is to the controlling ideas which guide and make each story unique, *All the Write Moves* reveals the essential elements that make up great stories and lets some authors rise above the crowd. You want your fiction to soar, so let's get started in making you the best storyteller you can be.

Author Bio:

Writer and teacher R. A. Paterson spent the last two decades teaching scriptwriting, business communications, and media studies at schools and colleges across Asia and North America. As a freelancer, he worked as an editor, scriptwriter, copywriter, and consultant on everything from novels to video games. However, it is his no-nonsense practical approach to writing skills that has helped so many of his students realize their dreams of turning their ideas into screenplays, comics, and novels. He is also the author of the novel *The Crocodile Princess*, currently under development as a feature film by Keller Entertainment.

By R.A. Paterson

Cover designed by pixelstudio

Robyn Paterson
Visit my website at www.robynpaterson.com

Printed in the United States of America

ISBN- 978-1-989357-00-2

DEDICATION

To my parents, the finest storytellers I know, and who instilled in me a love of storytelling and a desire to share it with the world.

With special thanks to:
Richard Moule for helping to inspire this book.
Don Chisholm for his shared wisdom.

And extra thanks to:
Chad Hicks, Yi Weng, Jack Ward, and my many writing students, who have taught me as much as I have taught them.

And finally, to my wife, Connie. For putting up with my clattering keys and late nights.

CONTENTS

AUTHOR'S FORWARD

When I wrote my first book on writing, Write! Shonen Manga, I made the choice to include a section in that book on the basics of writing stories. As a writing teacher, I was worried that some of my audience might not understand the art of crafting stories around manga without first understanding the basics of writing fiction as well.

As it turned out, the quick-start writing materials I included in that book proved to be just as popular as the in-depth materials on writing Japanese comic books, and so I decided to revise and expand that section into a book of its own. That is the book in front of you right now.

If you have already read the first edition of my book on writing manga, then most of this material will seem familiar to you, however this book contains several new chapters and I revised several of the old ones as well. Writing about writing, like writing itself, is a never-ending process, and new things are always coming up that are worth sharing. In many ways, writing this book was more about deciding what not to include than it was deciding what to include.

In any case, I hope this book is helpful to you in your journey as a writer.

R.A. Paterson

THE SHAKESPEARE CODE

If there is one desire in every new writer's heart, it is to find "The Shakespeare Code," and like the Bard himself be able to write stories that will entrance audiences and last the test of time. Storytellers through the ages have sought it like a Holy Grail, believing that out there lies a single secret formula which they can use like a magic spell to achieve literary success and acclaim. Even today, you can find Amazon.com filled with books with titles like "Write the Perfect Novel," "The Five Day Bestseller," and "Six Steps to the Perfect Screenplay."

Online, you can find countless articles that will give you checklists and collections of plot points and story beats that "can't fail to make your story soar!" These will be different depending on the genre and type of story, and while some are both helpful and inspiring, others leave readers scratching their heads.

Lines like, "At the structural junction of the conflict peristalsis, the hero must rip open their chest and bear their inner flawed heart to the world," have made many an aspiring author want to throw their tablet against the wall in frustration. And, the only thing that keeps saving their poor tablet is that somewhere deep down the author wonders if there is magic there that they're missing, and that if they can only harness it, their fiction will show the world what they can really do.

That's the Shakespeare Code, and the inner hunt for it in action. We desperately want to believe that it's out there, and think that if we can only find it our name will be up there next to Hemmingway, Steinbeck, Austin, and the other greats of the literary cannon.

But here's the truth- there is no Shakespeare Code.

There is no one magic formula that can turn your writing into gold and make the world worship you, no matter how many people try to sell you that there is. Instead, there are many, many different tricks and techniques that work for some writers and don't work for others. For every "perfect" formula that you'll find, there are tens of thousands of writers who won't be able to use it to save their lives, or their stories.

So, this book won't give you the perfect formula, because there isn't one.

What this book will give you is knowledge that's been handed down from one generation to the next by storytellers since the dawn of mankind. It will tell you the basic things you need to know to build your own path and find the way of telling stories that works best for you, no matter what kind of story you're trying to tell. In a practical, straightforward manner it will lay out the fundamental ideas that make fiction work, and show you what's worked for others who came before you.

In other words, this book isn't the Shakespeare Code- but it is the quick-start manual to building your own Shakespeare Code.

One that works for you and you alone, and lets your fiction rise above the rest.

Let's get started!

THE BUILDING BLOCKS OF STORY

A well-known scientist (some say it was Bertrand Russell) once gave a public lecture on astronomy. He described how the earth orbits around the sun and how the sun, in turn, orbits around the center of a vast collection of stars called our galaxy. At the end of the lecture, a little old lady at the back of the room got up and said: "What you have told us is rubbish. The world is really a flat plate supported on the back of a giant tortoise." The scientist gave a superior smile before replying, "What is the tortoise standing on?" "You're very clever, young man, very clever," said the old lady. "But it's turtles all the way down!" -Stephen Hawking, A Brief History of Time (1988)

WHAT IS A STORY?

It may surprise you to learn that all stories are mystery stories.

They're mysteries which seek to answer a very simple question- why did the results at the end of the story happen? And every step, every thing, which happens in a story is a trail of evidence that shows the audience the causes that produced that final effect.

Why was the little girl crying? She was the only one who didn't get an invitation to her friend's birthday party. Why didn't she get the invitation? She played a joke on one of her friends. Why did she play the joke? Her brother put her up to it. Why did her brother put her up to it? He was annoyed because she borrowed his baseball glove and ruined it. And so on- a chain of evidence that produces the effect at the end of the story, but in stories the audience usually watches them happen from the beginning to the end instead of the other way around.

Thus, there are three elements to every story, and for something to be considered a story it needs all three of these parts.

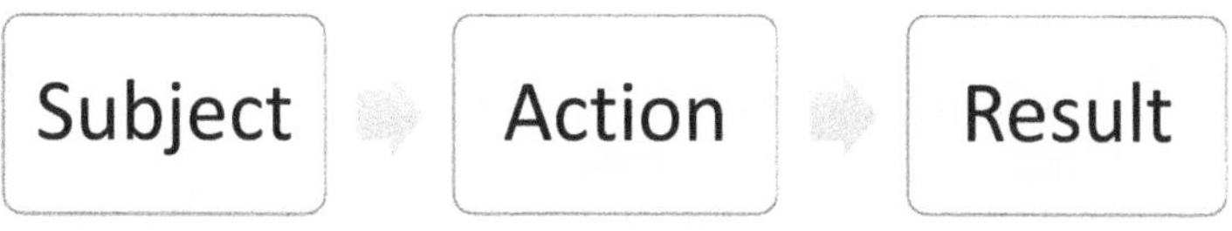

The Subject is the person or thing which is taking the action, or is on the receiving end of the action. If the subject is active (as most subjects in stories are), then they are the ones doing the action and usually working toward some result. If they're passive, then they're the ones who are being acted on by other people or things which may not be under their control. For example, a jogger practicing for a race is an active subject, while a candle melting in the sun is a passive one. Subjects can be implied rather than shown, if the writer is skilled enough, or they were already introduced.

The Action is something which the subject does, or which is done to the subject. The subject can be the giver, or they can be the receiver of the action. Even passivity is a choice, and thus qualifies as an action (not making a choice is still a choice, after all).

A Result is what happens because that action was taken. This is the part that's easy to forget, but it's really the most important part. Without a result, knowing about the subject and the action they took is pretty much useless, which is why endings are so important to a story. It is that you can see the results of something that turns activity into story, and the result is where the action comes together to form the ending of the narrative. In addition, the results which happen at the end of stories must be the consequences of actions taken to have meaning because it helps us to understand why things happen in the world around us- our brains are constantly seeking causes to go along with effects.

Together, these three things make a "story unit," which is the most basic form that a story can take and still be considered a story. If something includes these three elements, then our heads view it as a story, and potential knowledge, while if something is missing it just becomes information, but not a story.

Here's three examples:

1. Bob runs
2. Ali drinks
3. Jesi studies

In each of these, there is a subject (a person's name) and an action (verb) which tells us what that subject is doing. However, you will notice that none of these is a story, and you wouldn't call any of them stories the way they are. That's because they're missing the other key ingredient which a story unit requires- a result which happens from the subject performing that action.

1. Bob runs from the bull and gets away.
2. Ali drinks medicine and cures his stomach ache.
3. Jesi studies hard for her test and gets a perfect score.

Now do these look like stories to you? Yes, they're very simple stories, but with the addition of a result to go along with the subject and action taken you now have all the requirements met to call something a story. Everything you add on top of this is just more detailed information to make the story more interesting, entertaining or informative to the audience.

Not only that, one of the amazing things about story units is that they're infinitely flexible is both size and how you use them. For example, each of those three examples is a single story unit, but then so is all 1225 pages of Tolstoy's *War and Peace*. As long as there's a single greater action being taken which links all the events of a story together, a single work of fiction (or non-fiction) can be considered a single story unit. Also, smaller story units can be used to build larger ones, like LEGO bricks, with most scenes in a story being a single smaller story unit (or part of one), and even actions within a scene being made of up yet smaller story units.

No matter how much detail you look at a story in, or how far out you view the story from, if it's a story then it's made of story units.

Adding Details

As you might have noticed, each of those stories above is a bit boring. Yes, they tell the reader about a subject, action, and result, but human brains won't spend much time on them because there's not a lot they can learn from them. For a story to be useful, and thus interesting to people's brains, there needs to be details. Details are the spice that turn a simple story into a delicious meal of knowledge that has audiences coming back for more.

Here's another example:

- Bill studied for his history test and passed with a perfect score.

This is great for Bill, but could you do what Bill did based on just that information?

The answer is probably not. Because that story, while complete as a story, lacks details...

- Who did he study with?
- What did Bill study?
- Where did Bill study?
- When did Bill study?
- Why did Bill study what he did?
- How did Bill study?

All of these are important questions the audience needs to know to get the same results Bill did, and without knowing these things it becomes pretty difficult to learn anything from this story. You can make guesses, but the point of stories is to share information, and the more details audiences have to work with, the better.

The more audiences know, the more useful the story becomes. This is why our brains don't just want details- they crave them like you crave junk food. Details are the sweet stuff that our brains love, because they help humans to figure out what's useful and what's not, and they give us survival information.

So, what details do you need to include in a story?

The simplest way to add detail to a story and start to make it more interesting is by using the **5WH method**, which is something writers have been using for a long time when they plan their stories, and you can too!

How does it work?

Well, that's the best part- you already know it! You just need a bit of help remembering.

To use the 5WH method, you just need to answer the following questions:

- **Where** does the story happen?
- **When** does this story take place?
- **Who** is involved?
- **Why** do the characters do what they do?

- **What** happens? What goes wrong (or right)?
- **How** does it all turn out?

Let's look at an example based on Bill's story.

Bill (who) wanted to get a good score on his history test (why), so he recopied out his notes at home (what, where), had a group study session with his friends after class (what, when), and asked the teacher some extra questions (what). As a result, he got a perfect score on the test. (How it turned out.)

Now, could you do what Bill did and get a good score?

The truth is, almost anyone could.

You might notice that not all of the questions are answered in the same order as above, and that's normal. Also, some questions are answered more than once, and that's okay too. The important thing is that you answer as many of them as you can, because the more details you include the more interesting people will find the story.

<u>But only include the details that are important to understanding the point of the story.</u>

So, if the point of the story is to show how you can get a great test score like Bill did, then the details of the story are going to be about things related to his studies. They're not going to be about how he took a nap, or sang Karaoke, or how he asked his classmate on a date. Those might be things that happened while he was studying for the test, but they're not relevant to the story. All they would do is clutter the story and make it confusing and unclear to the reader what the story is about.

Everything in the story must be connected to the main point or ideas of the story, and more specifically, it must all be connected to the Spine of Action...

THE IMPORTANCE OF THE SPINE OF ACTION

The Spine of Action is the central action that a story unit is built around- the thing that holds the whole story together and gives it a sense of unity. Without it, just like a person without a real spine, the story will fall apart or just turn into a shapeless blob. Stories need a skeleton to hold them together, and the Spine of Action provides that very important piece of structure.

The Spine of Action...

- Tells us where the head of the story is- the subject/start.
- Connects the parts of the story together – the actions.
- Shows us where the bottom of the story is- the result/ending.

Let's look at the example of studious Bill to see this in action.

- Bill studied for his History test and passed with a perfect score.

In this story, the key words here are "studied for his history test," which represents the Spine of Action for this story. This means that everything in the story must be linked to Bill, and his studying for that history test, from the things he does to the details of how he does them.

So, the actions of the more detailed version...

1. Bill wanted to get a good score on his history test
2. So, he recopied out his notes at home,
3. Had a group study session with his friends after class,
4. And asked the teacher some extra questions.
5. As a result, he got a perfect score on the test.

All make sense, because they're connected to that central goal/point of studying for the history test and getting a good score. However, if you were to add some other actions...

1. Bill wanted to get a good score on his history test
2. So, he recopied out his notes at home
3. He also took a nap
4. Then he sang Karaoke
5. And, he had a group study session with his friends after class
6. And also asked the teacher some extra questions.
7. Finally, he asked his classmate on a date
8. As a result, he got a perfect score on the test.

Now instead of Bill's very clear and simple story, you have a messy and unclear story where the audience can see some things fit, but now has to wonder how the other things are connected. (Short answer- they're not.) Naps, karaoke and dating are great for Bill, but unless they affect the story in some way, they don't belong in this story, and should be left out.

However, the Spine of Action doesn't just tell you what to leave out, it also tells you what to include. Since you know where the story starts and ends, you now have a clear map that shows you your beginning and your destination, now all you need to do is plot your route between those two points.

Every major action has a bunch of little actions or steps that go with it- things that you have to do to accomplish that goal. So, once you know what your story's Spine of Action is, you just need to sit down and think about the way your character is going to try and accomplish that goal.

How the character does it will be mostly determined by the character, story, and circumstances, so the bad news is there's no single magic formula for doing this. On the other hand, the good news is that there's no single way to do it! Whatever way you have your character do it, is the right way for that character, or wrong way if it doesn't work out.

For example, let's say the main character is Lisa, and Lisa wants to get her driver's license.

The first thing you'd need to do is sit down and think about what steps someone goes through to get their driver's license. Typically, you need to go take a written test to get your learner's permit, then you need to practice driving for a while, and then finally you can take the test. So, breaking it down you can see what looks like one action "Getting the driver's license" is actually three actions.

1. Write written test.
2. Practice driving.
3. Take driving test.

Now you know what the three major parts of Lisa's story are, and if you add a beginning and ending, you get...

1. Lisa decides to get her license so she can drive to the beach
2. She writes the written test to get her learner's permit.
3. She practices driving.
4. She takes the driving test.
5. She passes the test and drives to the beach.

Here, you have a complete story about Lisa getting her license, and you know what the major steps of the story are going to be. Of course, you don't have to include all the steps of a process in a story, just the ones which are most interesting and which reflect your story's point, and you can leave some steps out or spend more time with some steps than others.

For example, if you want to tell a story which focuses on how Lisa is afraid of driving at first, then most of the story's focus will be spent on the driving practice part, and the final test will be where you show that she's overcome her fear. You won't spend a lot of time on the written test because that's not related to her fear of being behind the wheel.

Remember the golden rule of storytelling- While details are important, only include important details. The brains of your audience only want to know what they need to know to understand why the character's main action succeeded or failed at the end, they don't want to know what your character posted on Facebook, unless it's connected to the story.

The Spine of Action and Plot

So, how are the Spine of Action and the Plot connected?

Simply put, the Plot is the path the character takes to achieve the results of their Spine of Action.

You see, actions come in all shapes and sizes, and what looks like one single action is often actually a bunch of smaller actions in disguise.

For example, let's say you're baking a cake.

Is baking a cake a single action?

No, it's not. If you want to bake a cake you need to...

1. **Gather** the ingredients.
2. **Pre-heat** the oven.
3. **Mix** the dry ingredients and wet ingredients.
4. **Combine** the wet ingredients with the dry ingredients.
5. **Grease** the cake pan.
6. **Pour** the batter in the pan.
7. **Put** the cake in the oven.
8. **Set** the timer.
9. **Watch** the cake to make sure it doesn't get overdone.
10. **Check** the cake with a toothpick to see if it's done.
11. **Take** the cake out.
12. **Turn** off the oven.
13. **Put** the cake on a cooling rack.
14. **Ice** the cake.

We use the broad action term "bake a cake" to describe making a cake, but as you can see, inside that unassuming phrase "bake a cake" you have over fourteen different actions being taken. (And this is a simplified list, there are actually many more!) And, there are many different ways to carry out these steps, with different bakers doing them in diverse ways.

That's where plot comes in.

The plot of a story is an organized pattern of events which come together to form a story. It is the way in which the writer has the characters or events navigate their way through the possible options created by the Spine of Action to reach the story's ending.

To continue the cake example, if one baker wants to create an Angel Food Cake, they will use slightly different ingredients and baking methods, while another baker who wants to make a Marble Layer Cake will follow yet another approach. Both of them have the same goal of baking a cake, and both of them are following the above steps in similar order, but they're doing it another way because they want different results at the end.

In a similar way, each detective in a murder mystery story follows the procedure of gathering evidence and searching for information differently, even though they all have the same goal- solve the murder. How they solve that murder, and the way in which they achieve their goals is the plot of the story, and is what makes each murder mystery novel unique. They all have the same Spine of Action, but the way in which they thread that Spine of Action, the plot, is what makes them different.

In another example, a Romance story is about how two people come together, navigate the challenges of a relationship, and find happiness with each other. Almost all Romance stories have these common elements, which fall under the broad action term "fall in love." However, as everyone who has been in a relationship knows, many, many smaller actions and events happen between a couple meeting and a couple committing to each other. These actions and events might play out over years, weeks, days, hours or even minutes, but they need to happen for the couple to build a working relationship or it will fall apart.

How that couple navigates those choices and the unexpected events which occur (both good and bad), are what makes up the plot of the story, and expands on the simple idea of "falling in love."

It also creates the framework which everything else in the story is built around- characters, setting, events, and theme are all things that will be built around the structure which has been created by the plot. It will be the thing that shapes them, guides them, and holds them all together as a single coherent story. One example of this is the three-act structure.

STORY UNITS EXPANDED- THE THREE-ACT STRUCTURE

The concept of breaking a story down into three phases isn't new, and is so natural that in his book *Poetics* from 335 BC, the Greek Philosopher Aristotle proposed that all dramas could be broken up into a beginning, middle, and end, and that each of the phases had their own natural characteristics. This story structure would later become referred to as the three-act structure, partly because in Aristotle's time the dramas were broken down into "acts," which were brief pauses in the drama to allow for costume and scene changes.

What Aristotle had hit upon, however, wasn't just a better way of looking at writing drama, but the fundamental basic building blocks of storytelling itself. All stories, no matter how short or long, can be broken down into the three clear phases of a story unit, which aren't just a three-part structure, but a three-act structure which not only tells us how things happen, but what needs to happen at that phase of the story for it to be a story.

As was covered above, the basic elements of a story unit are subject-action-result, however when you're expanding this out to cover a complete story you need to make a small change. Instead of subject-action-result, the three-act structure is better understood as **setup**-action-result. The reason that "subject" needs to be replaced with "setup" is to make clear that that you're not just talking about the person or thing acting (or being acted on), you're talking about all the information the audience needs to know to understand everything that comes after it.

Let's look at the three-act structure in more detail to understand exactly what each part does.

Act 1: Setup → Act 2: Action → Act 3: Result

Act 1: Setup (aka the Situation, Introduction, or Beginning)

Length: usually between the first 10% to 35% of the story, averaging 25%.

Questions Answered: Who is involved? Where are they? When does this take place? What motivates them? Why are they doing what they're doing?

Details:

The first phase of any story unit exists to tell the audience everything they're going to need to know to understand the rest of the story. This doesn't just include characters, time, place, and other matters of context, but it also includes the motivations and problems that the characters face. The story begins here with a character and a goal or need, and this will be the central idea that carries the story from here to the end.

Notes:

- Act One should always introduce some problem the main character must deal with, even if it's just that they're thirsty. Whether it's a single sentence or a whole series, the character should be given a motivator like a need or goal which guides them and makes them get off their sofa, put down their phone, and take action.
- Act One doesn't have to be the "real" first part of the story, it's just the point where you drop your audience into the story. The story itself often started long before the main characters or audience get involved, and the first part is about playing catch-up while the action is already in progress. However, this is still the first part of the story you're telling because it's still performing a setup function. In cases like this, the first act might only be as long as 10% of the story because the author wants to get the characters and audience up to speed as soon as possible and get on with the action.
- Nothing should happen in the story which isn't laid out in some way during the first act. It might not be directly shown, but everything that happens should be a natural outgrowth of controlling ideas and story elements which are presented to the audience in the first part. If there's a storm in the Third Act/Result phase, clouds should be gathering in the First Act/Setup phase.
- Villains sometimes aren't shown directly in the first Act of a longer story, but their presence is hinted at in some way or suggested by the situation.
- Story Guru Michael Hague often remarks that "all story problems can ultimately be traced back to the first act." He's right, so think through your Setup phase carefully, and look here when you have problems writing later parts of the story.

Act 2: Action (aka the Development, Conflict, Event, or Confrontation)

Length: extremely flexible, but usually the middle 40%-80% of the story, averaging 50%.

Questions Answered: What happens? How does the main character try to solve the problem? What gets in their way? How do they overcome challenges?

Details:

The middle phase of any story is where most of the story's action is going to take place. The main character of the story unit tries to accomplish some goal, and may or may not make progress towards achieving that goal. They may succeed, fail, meet resistance, or discover new information which complicates the situation and changes or modifies their goal. There are many possibilities, which is why this phase is so flexible in length. The main requirements for the Act Two/Action phase are that it's interesting to the audience and that everything that happens is an extension of what was introduced in the Act One/Setup phase.

Notes:

- Typically, most stories are conflict based, which means that they're about a character in conflict with themselves, another person, society, or the world around them. In these stories, the Action phase is where the character comes into conflict with a someone or something that prevents them from accomplishing their goals. Whether they succeed or fail is left for the Result phase to decide.
- The Act Two/Action phase often ends with some kind of twist or dramatic turn that changes the situation (often for the worse) and increases the level of drama going into the Result phase.
- For more on how keep your audience engaged during the Action phase, see the Engagement section in the chapter on Controlling Ideas and the Plot chapter of the book,

Act 3: Result (aka the Resolution, Denouement, Climax, or Ending)

Length: usually the final 10%-30% of the story, averaging 25%.

Questions Answered: How does it all turn out? Does the main character succeed or fail? How do they accomplish (or fail to accomplish) their goals? What happens to them after the story is done? What are the consequences of the actions they took in the story?

Details:

The end Result phase of any story is there to bring everything to a satisfying close. It usually contains the climax, where the main character takes one last try at accomplishing their goals, and the ending, where you see the results of everything the main character did come together.

Notes:

- Audiences want satisfying endings more than surprise endings, and a satisfying ending is one which is logical and earned by the main character. It is the result of the actions taken in the story, the choices they made, and feels "right" to the audience based on everything which has taken place.
- If possible, endings should also surprise the audience in some way for the best dramatic effect, but surprise is less important than satisfaction. The audience knows all along the main character will generally succeed and wants

it to happen (at least at the end of the story), but they also want to know how the character does it and see it happen in an interesting way.

- There should be no major loose ends (unless the story is part of a larger one), and everything introduced in the Act One/Setup phase should be resolved in the Act Three/Result phase. Chekov's Gun should always be respected.

You might have noticed that this explanation of the three-act structure is a bit simple and vague, and that's on purpose. For you see, everything written above is meant to be used at different levels of the story, not just the overall story most writers think of. After all, the three-act structure is present whether it's a single scene, a sequence, a story arc, a full work like a novel or film, a series, or a serial- all of these levels of story are using the three-act structure, from top to bottom. Let's take a look at each to see how...

SCENES

The main building block of stories is the scene, which is where you tell what happens to a particular set of subjects at a particular time and place. The subjects could be candles, people or roosters- it doesn't matter just so long as they're the focus of an action or the cause of an action, and you watch it play out. Scenes, like all pieces of a story, are actually mini-stories themselves which still follow the three-act structure of setup-action-result, but this isn't always obvious because some parts can sometimes be implied rather than shown or broken up across multiple scenes.

Here is a typical scene structure:

Act 1: Setup

In this case, setup means situation- which involves telling the audience what they need to know to understand what's going to happen in this scene. At minimum, they usually need to know who is in the scene, when it takes place, where they are, and what they want. They might also need to know why the characters are doing what they're doing, so they have some idea of the character's motivations.

Keep in mind that if these things are already established in the minds of the audience, the audience doesn't need to be told them again. The audience only needs to be told what's changed, or be reminded of what they need to know but might have forgotten because time has passed.

Act 2: Action

Once the situation is (re)established, then the characters in the scene will try to complete their goals. What those goals are, and how they go about trying to complete them, will depend on the characters and the writer. These might be scene goals, which means they're something the character is trying to do because of what's happening in that scene, or these might be part of the main story's Spine of Action.

In either case, the characters should be trying to do it in a way which is interesting to the audience because you never want to bore your audience. What happens should reflect the characters, the situations they're in, the conflicts of the story, and anything else that needs to be there. But, regardless at the heart of the scene is characters trying to do something for their own reasons.

Act 3: Result

At some point, the characters are going to either accomplish their goals or they aren't. If a scene is self-contained, at the end of a story, or the end of a story arc, then the characters might successfully accomplish whatever it is they're trying to do. However, more commonly, the characters will accomplish a smaller goal which is only part of a bigger one (but still have more to do), or they'll outright fail in accomplishing their goals and be forced to regroup and try again.

Remember that characters accomplishing goals reduces the level of interest in a story, while characters not accomplishing goals increases audience interest. So, writing successful scenes is actually about not giving the audience what they want (which is the character to succeed), but instead keeping the character active and trying to accomplish goals.

A very common trick when writing scenes is to have them end before the story of the scene is completely resolved as a way to keep the reader reading. For example, the scene might reach its climax where the main character has asked a boy to the dance, but the scene ends before you hear his reply. The answer will be given in another scene, usually at the start of the scene where you find out the new situation the character is in as a result of the results of that previous scene. This might be an active scene where she is planning what to wear to the dance, or a reactive scene where she thinks her life is over at 16 and she's going to die old and alone. Either way, the reader will want to know what happens, and you'll carry them into another story-scene, and then another, and another, until the dawn comes up and they realize they've been reading the whole night.

That's how you write something they can't put down.

SEQUENCES

Sometimes stories run for multiple scenes, in which case they're called sequences. A sequence is a series of scenes which connect together to form a single complete story unit. It might be two scenes, or it might take place over a hundred scenes, but together they form a complete story. However, this story isn't the main story, but a smaller story within a larger one. It might be a car chase, or a training montage, a fight sequence, or a flashback to a series of historical events, but together these scenes tell another smaller story within a larger one.

The only requirements to a sequence are that it has a clear beginning and ending, and these are linked in some way by the events and actions which connect them in the ensuing scenes. For example, a simple car chase sequence might start when the police officers see the escaping bank robbers, involve a highway chase, a marketplace chase, and even switch to being a boat chase at the end, but when the police catch the bad guys (or they can no longer pursue them) the sequence ends.

Similarly, a sequence's scenes don't have to be connect directly by time and place. A sequence of a man asking a woman to marry him might start a high school in Minnesota, happen next at the University of Hawaii several years later, jump to a proposal in Egypt atop a pyramid a decade after that, take place next in Paris when they're middle aged, and finally end when she accepts on her seventy-fifth birthday floating in orbit. It's still a sequence which has a beginning-middle-end, and which is linked by the thread of the man proposing to the woman he loves (and getting rejected).

Lastly, sequences can have other sequences intermixed with them or happen within them. Sequences can even be made up of other smaller sequences! A character's personal background flashback sequence might consist of a sequence of them struggling with math as a child, another sequence of them getting their PhD in physics, and then finally a sequence of them creating a new power source that transforms the world. Each is a part of their larger sequence of them becoming the person they are today in the greater story being told.

Similarly, a popular tactic for writers to keep the tension on in stories is to have two or more sequences happening at the same time that involve different characters and jump back and forth between them. This is especially useful if one character's sequence is dramatic and exciting while the other character's sequence is less dramatic but still important to the story. This way, the dramatic sequence keeps the audience engaged and reading, while the less dramatic one creates pauses and builds tension as it plays out between the more dramatic scenes.

Story A, Scene 1	→	Story B, Scene 1	→	Story A, Scene 2	→	Story B, Scene 2	→	Story A, Scene 3	→	Story B, Scene 3	→	And so on...

It goes without saying that typically the scenes which make up a sequence are still using the three-act structure themselves, but being part of a sequence lets a writer play with that more. Scenes within a sequence often skip establishing the situation and assume the audience already knows it, so they only need to tell the audience what's changed since the last scene and go from there. Similarly, sequences often break down the actions the characters take over multiple scenes, like a fight sequence where first the hero attacks, then the bad guy responds, and then the hero tries again but the bad guy gets the upper hand, and so on. Each is a part of the greater sequence of "a fight," but still broken down into smaller scenes of action.

STORY ARCS

Story Arcs are longer stories which play out on the higher and lower levels of the story than sequences. On the lower level, a Story Arc might involve one character who is going through their own story inside a larger story, with the actions they take being told within the scenes of another character's story. For example, in a book about a heroic crusading reporter trying to bring down a corrupt politician, they might have a sidekick rookie character fresh out of college who is helping them. The rookie is learning to face their fears and ask questions under the guidance of the main character (the heroic one), but the rookie's story isn't the main story of the book. The rookie's growth and change are a Story Arc, and are happening inside the bigger story which isn't actually about them.

On the other hand, Story Arcs can also operate at the highest levels, happening over multiple books in a series or episodes of a TV drama. Each episode contains a small piece of the larger story, with the story arcs being woven inside the larger stories and helping to tie them together. For example, in a disaster novel series about survival, a character might also have a story arc where he is trying to find his sister that was separated from him during the crisis. The main story is about how the character survives the disaster, but his search for his sister is a story happening inside that larger story that is ongoing as the series plays out and eventually comes to some resolution.

ACTS

The three-act structure, is of course also known as the three-act structure, because that's how it was originally used back in Aristotle's time. He saw it as being a beginning-middle-end trio, but over the years many writers have played with it and expressed it in different ways. Other ways to describe the Act 1-Act 2-Act 3 phases are "setup-action-reaction," "thesis-antithesis-synthesis," and "introduction-conflict-resolution." However, no matter what the form or length of the story, ultimately the three-act structure is always there lurking underneath the surface, and those same three key elements that make up a story unit are there along with it.

That said, while the parts of a three-act story unit must always be present when the story is finished, the order in which they're presented in doesn't always have to be fixed or chronological. For example, a common writing trick to get stories right into the action is to start with what is actually Act Two of the greater story, give the audience the Act One information during a lull in the action, and then continue right on with Act Two and Act Three as per normal.

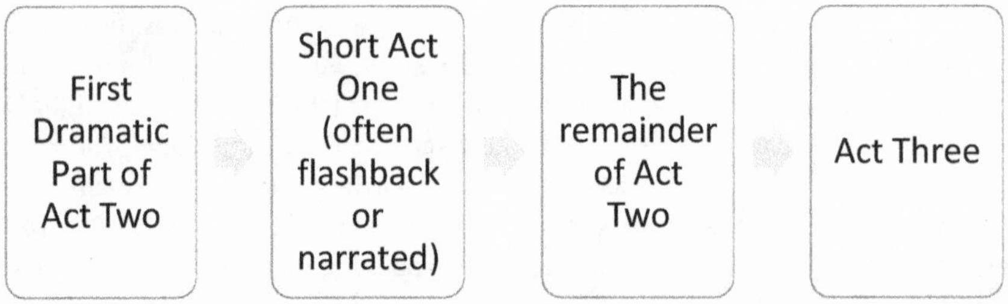

First Dramatic Part of Act Two

Short Act One (often flashback or narrated)

The remainder of Act Two

Act Three

Or, for shorter or episodic fiction, writers sometimes start with an exciting part from Act Three, then jump back in time to Act One and tell the story events which lead up to that dramatic moment in Act Three.

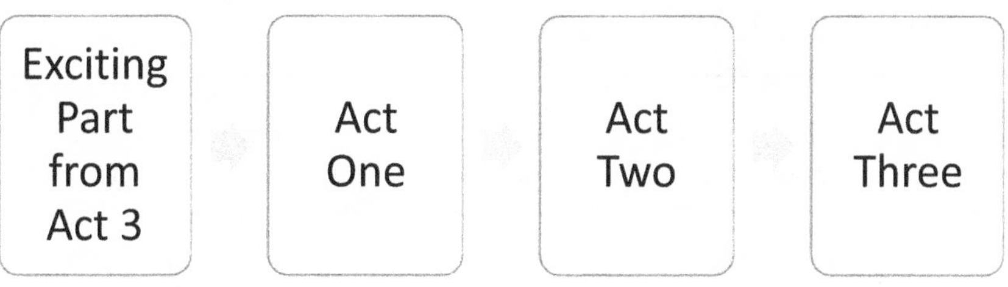

Both are ways to catch the reader's attention and keep them curious about what caused these dramatic events to happen.

Thus, as you can see, while each part of a three-act story unit has certain functions and questions it answers for the audience, that doesn't mean that a writer can't move some of those to other acts to achieve dramatic effects or heighten curiosity. For instance, the main character's motivation for doing what they do might not be revealed until the end of the story, or the answers to how the main character overcomes the challenges of Act Two/Action might not be revealed until the end of Act Three/Result. As long as the writer includes all the pieces the audience needs to understand the story somewhere (and doesn't confuse their audience too much) they can feel free to play with the story however they want.

Those of you who have studied writing might have come across other story structures, such as ones which claim 4, 5, 7, 11, 18, or even 36 "acts", and wonder how those fit in with the three-act structure. The reality is that those other story structures are actually still just three-act structures, but different writing teachers or writers have split them into smaller acts for their own reasons. For example, some writers break Act One/Setup into two smaller phases which first introduce the characters and situations, and then introduce a problem which will be the central challenge for the story. This might be presented as two acts, but in reality they're just the single introductory act split into two.

If you find for your own writing that you prefer to subdivide the three-act structure into smaller pieces to create a formula that works for you, then do it! Just remember that any divisions of the Three Act Structure are just tricks to make writing easier or more efficient for a particular type of writing, they're not actually different from the basic three-act structure, which is always there in some form.

Check out the "Plot as Structure" section in the Plot chapter for several examples of different takes on the three-act structure, which show several of the most common ways to break stories down. At the same time, check out the "Plot Formulas" section to see several common plots laid out in more detail for different types of stories.

SERIES AND SERIALS

A Series – This describes a collection of books, movies, television episodes, or comic issues where the individual parts are mostly self-contained story units. Once upon a time, they would literally be self-contained stories and there would be few to no connections between the individual books or TV episodes because it was hard for audiences to see past episodes or find past volumes. However, in the last few decades there's been a shift to storytelling where story arcs are allowed to run across multiple volumes, and even episodic TV series usually have story arcs playing across entire seasons. This keeps audiences coming back, and makes the stories feel larger and more epic. Naturally, the story arcs which play out across the many smaller parts are all based on the three-act structure, and the whole season or series of books will represent a complete story.

A Serial – A serial is a long story where the whole thing is one giant story, but which is usually broken down into chapters, episodes, sequences, or story arcs that may be smaller story units. However, unlike a series, a serial's stories are all connected to each other and often can't be read easily without reading what came before or afterwards. This was fiction's original form, as newspapers and magazines often ran serial fiction dating back into the 1700s as a way to keep readers buying the next issue. Typically, each chapter or episode of a serial ends on a dramatic note that requires the reader to read the next part to find out what happens next. The most common version of this is that serial chapters tend to end with Act Two of a story unit (or the Climax of Act Three), and then start each new story unit by resolving Act Three from the previous story unit before beginning the next story unit. In this way, the story requires the audience to keep reading to find out what happens next right until the end.

Final Notes on the Three-Act Structure

Thus, you can see that the three-act structure is the basic form of all storytelling, from top to bottom. It's the expanded version of the subject-action-result story unit that we use to tell more complex stories, and which gains its power from its simplicity and universality. Just like the turtles in Professor Hawking's apocryphal story, stories use the three-act structure from top to bottom, and mastering one level of it lets you begin to unlock the others as well.

Think about it. Play with it. Make it the heart of your writing until it's the most natural thing in the world, and your stories will always have an underlying structure that keeps them on track to a proper end.

CHANGE- THE FINAL BUILDING BLOCK OF STORYTELLING.

A common piece of wisdom among writing teachers is that stories are all about character change, and all good stories are about lead characters who grow and transform as the story plays out. You will find this advice everywhere from books to online, and in many writing circles it's taken as gospel that this is the one true way to write a story.

It's a piece of advice which has also brought great amusement to generations of mystery, action, pulp, television, and superhero comic writers who have cashed big monthly cheques for writing stories where the main character didn't change even a tiny bit.

So no, not all stories are about the main character going on some great heroic journey of personal transformation.

But, the writing gurus are right about one thing: change is an important and necessary part of stories, and in fact all stories should contain at least some attempt at change. The part where they go wrong is assuming that it can only be the lead character that changes, when in fact the change can come in one of three different forms- lead character change, secondary character change, or setting change.

Lead Character Change

This is where the lead character undergoes what is usually called a "character arc," where they start the story as one type of person and they finish the story as another. This might be small changes, like their opinion on pineapple on pizza going from hating it to liking it, or it might be a major change like going from a hateful miser to being a generous and loving man. Usually the main character starts their story with one clear position, and through the events of the story they are given a reason to change their position to something else. Typically, this change is caused by things external to the character, and they wouldn't have wished it if they had a choice, but it happens and they change because of it. Also, characters, like real people, like who they are, and don't like to change easily, so it often takes a real boot in the pants to get them to change. The bigger the change, the bigger the boot in the pants required to get them to make it.

Secondary Character Change

Like the lead character, the characters around them from opponents to allies, can also undergo character arcs. These arcs of change may be major or minor, and will see them changing as characters in some part of their lives. Very often, if the lead character doesn't change in a story, there is a secondary character (usually an ally, but sometimes an enemy) who changes instead, with the lead character being the cause of that change, or a window for the audience to see it happen. This might be a character who was inspired to change by watching the lead character take action, or who was transformed by the events which take place from one person into another. One common trick in action stories is to make them about the villain, and have the villain be the one who is undergoing the character arc while the hero is there to stop them when it all goes bad. However, this can just as easily be someone the hero helps, and in the process that that character learns from the hero and changes accordingly.

Setting Change

Finally, it is perfectly possible to have a story where no character actually changes at all, but the world around them does in some way. A classic example of the world changing can be found in murder mystery stories, where the murder upsets the social order, and the detective character restores it by solving the crime (returning the world to what it was before the murder). Other examples of setting change could include a character whose actions cause social unrest, or a teacher who transforms a classroom from a dirty and chaotic one to a clean and ordered one. This change can be a big one, or a small one, and may or may not happen at the same time as character change. It may also be the result of characters trying to change the world, or a side effect of the characters trying to do other things, but the change happens nonetheless.

In any case, whether the change is character or setting, the story must at least imply, or explain, why the change happened and show a series of events which produced it. Those events may be directly about the change itself, or the things which cause the change may be something which happens in the background of the "real" story. The key is that the audience must be able to see some pattern of causes which produces the effects they see at the end of the story for it be satisfying. If you don't answer the question of why the change that happens occurs, then the audience will feel there is something wrong with the story, even if they can't quite put their finger on what it is.

So, to make stories satisfying, always make sure you understand the role change plays in them, and how the results at the end of the story fit with everything that comes before. Like all good mysteries, the audience wants to be able to see the trail of clues that leads to the satisfying conclusion. That's the key to writing a fulfilling ending that everyone will want to read.

CONTROLLING IDEAS

Imagine you were given the following things:

- A large blank sheet of white paper.
- A pencil.
- Four pennies.
- Two 6-sided dice.

Then, you and your friends were told to play a game with those things.

What would you do?

Many people would probably draw some lines on the paper, divide it into squares, and then pick one end of the squares as a starting point and the other end as an ending point. After that, they'd put the pennies on the starting square, and start rolling the dice to see how many squares each person's penny would move. They'd take turns doing this according to a set of rules that say each person gets a chance to move their penny, and that the first person to reach the end wins- turning the whole thing into a race to the finish line.

Or, perhaps you'd cut the paper in two, make paper airplanes with it, write your names on the side with the pencil and use the pennies as markers to create a goal zone to land the plane in. Then you could use the dice to decide who got the first turn at flying their plane, with the rules being that whoever managed to fly their plane over the goal three times won.

The fact is, you could come up with many different games with those simple materials- the only limits would be your imagination and the materials themselves.

And that, is exactly what you're doing when you write a story.

You tell the audience, "Here are the materials I'm going to work with." And then, you use the genre, characters, plots, setting and ideas of your story to show off what you and your imagination can create. Just like in a game, you set the playing board up, you agree on a set of rules, and then you use those things to present a story to your audience.

Perhaps it will be a small drama playing out at a single table at a restaurant between two people on a date, or maybe it will be a galactic epic set against the backdrop of a million solar systems and involving a cast of thousands- it doesn't matter. All that matters is that you start by telling your audience the boundaries of the story you're going to tell, and what can and can't happen in your story.

Because, like a board game, stories are not built on unlimited creativity, but instead built on limitations.

The moment you start to tell a story, you are limiting what can and will happen in that story.

And that's a good thing.

Because neither you nor the audience actually wants a story where anything can happen. You want a story where a particular set of people, in a particular situation, face a particular set of challenges, and arrive at a particular conclusion. After all, a story where anything can happen has no focus and no rules, and reading a story like that is no more fun than playing a game without logic or rules is. This is especially true since stories are actually a tool that we as humans use to learn about the world around us, and the real world has rules, so stories must as well if they're to be useful to us.

In writing fiction, there is a special set of rules that we call "controlling ideas", and they're the foundation around which a story is built. We use them to help set the limits to our stories so that the audience understands what's possible and what's not possible, and so that the author knows where they can go and where they can't. They also help to make our stories different from other stories told by other people, because while there are a limited number of possible stories and situations, there are an infinite number of controlling ideas we can play with to make those stories original and unique.

So, how to find your story's controlling ideas?

Well, let's look at a few ways to think about what kind of story you want to tell.

STORY GOALS

First, every story begins with a character, a goal, and an attempt to achieve that goal. It doesn't matter, whether it's the story itself, or the telling of a story, it's always true.

When you begin telling the story, you need to have a goal. You need to know why you are telling the story, and what you are trying to accomplish with it. Everything else flows from that- story, theme, dramatic questions, characters, setting, plot, and even your relationship with the audience. Everything in a story flows out of one central thing - the goal of the writer.

So, when you begin a project, always ask yourself- why am I writing this?

For example, your goal might be something like:

- I want the audience to feel really scared.
- I want to make the audience laugh.
- I want to show the audience how cool martial arts are.
- I want the audience to buy merchandise.
- I want the audience to protect the whales.
- I want to teach the audience about physics.

Whether you have one goal or many doesn't matter, nor does it matter how clear those goals are, but what does matter is that you have a goal. If you do, then you can use that goal to build and shape your story into reality. Your plans might change along the way, or your way of seeing the story might change, but as long as the goal itself is consistent, the story will be consistent, and your story will have a point.

And all stories need a point.

A point is what separates your story from random chatter without focus or direction. It's the thing that makes a story a story, and not just a list of facts or events. People tell stories for a reason, and that reason is the point of the story. It may be as sharp as a laser-honed blade, or as dull as a rock, but there needs to be a point in there somewhere. Otherwise, why would the audience bother to pay attention to your story at all?

This is the other major reason for knowing your goal- it lets you make your story into something that will accomplish your goal while still providing a clear focus that lets you and the audience know where it's going. After all, having a goal isn't enough, you need to have a plan for how you're going to achieve that goal.

The point is most often linked to a theme or argument that the writer is trying to make in the story itself (although not always), and is the way in which the writer's point is expressed through the story. So, for example:

- I want the audience to feel really scared- so I will tell a horror story about an alien virus taking over a small town and turning people insane and blind.
- I want to make the audience laugh- so I will tell a funny joke about two men in a tent.
- I want to show the audience how cool martial arts are- so I will tell a story about a female martial artist wandering a post-apocalyptic landscape protecting innocents and beating up raiders.

- I want the audience to buy merchandise- so I will tell a story based on popular trends that's filled with characters, catch phrases and symbols that can easily be turned into products.
- I want the audience to protect the whales- so I will tell a touching story about a boy trying to rescue a whale trapped in a cove and return it to the sea to create empathy towards whales.
- I want to teach the audience about physics- so I will tell the story of a man trapped on a space station using physics to plot his survival.

Each of these goals now has a plan attached to it, a way in which the writer intends to achieve that goal in the form of a story or way of writing a story. If you have these two things- a goal and a plan – you have the core seed of a story that can grow and flourish while still having a clear direction about where the story will go. Everything which follows in developing the story will build upon this goal and this plan.

You could even stop there and write the story, if you were so inclined.

However, that would be a bad idea, because the more you know about your story, and its controlling ideas, the better your story is going to be. So, let's look at a few other tools you can use (or not) to make your story's controlling ideas into a solid plan that will produce the story you want to write, and the story your audience wants to read.

ORIGINALITY

One of the most common things writers obsess over is originality.

But, there are two unhappy truths every writer must come to face if they want to be a writer:

1. It's all been done before.
2. People don't actually want original stories.

First, stories are about human beings, and while there are billions of people who have lived or are alive on Earth, human beings are still human beings. There are a limited number of possible stories and situations that human beings can face in their lives, and that includes stories involving magic, high technology, and other fantastic things. The ancient peoples of India were writing about great heroes using magic powers to duel demons in the *Ramayana* and high technology like flying machines in the *Mahābhārata* while the Roman Empire flourished. And even the Greek Philosopher Aristotle in 3rd Century BCE was commenting on how stories were all the same in his book *Poetics* when he wrote that all stories could be classified as man versus man, man versus himself, and man versus nature.

So, at some point, every writer needs to learn to just give up the idea that their stories are going to be something nobody has seen before- they're not, and they can't be. You can always find a version of any story in other places, and it's probably been told before in many different ways.

However, before you let this depress you, you should know something- Shakespeare, the man considered to be the father of so much of English culture and literature, was just taking the ancient Greek and Roman plays he'd read and making his own versions of them. The stories he thrilled audiences with weren't new, but he's remembered for how he presented them and the ways he changed the stories. In other words, while you can't really tell a new story, you can tell it your way, and by telling it your way, you can make it fresh, original, and your own.

And that's where you have a huge advantage- you're you, and nobody else on the planet is you. Nobody sees the world exactly like you do, nobody thinks exactly like you do, has eaten the same food, has the same family and friends, goes to the same schools, does the same job, or has loved the same people.

You and your life are unique among over seven billion people alive right now, and that automatically makes whatever story you tell unique, as long as you put some of yourself into it. Other people will find your story interesting exactly because you are the one telling it, and your life is different than theirs.

Therefore, becoming a writer, and a good one, is about finding out what makes your perspective special and using that to share your views with the world. Writing is about developing your own style and way of doing things, and then using that writer's voice to express yourself and your singular perspective through story. That's why you'll often hear the writing advice "write what you know," because only you can write your story, and your perspective is what will make your stories unique.

The second hard truth is that audiences already know what they want from stories- they want the things they already like, but in a slightly different way to keep it fresh.

Think about yourself.

When you finish a good book (or comic, or TV show, or movie, or video game...) that you loved and made you feel incredible, is your first thought- "Now, I want something that is nothing like what I just enjoyed!"

No, of course not. Your first thought is, "Give me more of that! What can I find what will give me the feeling I just got from this thing I love?"

Well, that's how almost everybody feels.

So, if you want to build an audience, your job as a writer isn't to give the audience something new, because that's not what they want- it's to give them something old but just different enough to make it feel new. They don't want completely new, because completely new is scary and unknown and they don't know if they'll like it, but if you give them something familiar with just a little twist, they'll accept it without hesitation.

How do you come up with that twist?

You draw from your own experiences, imagination, and stories that you've loved, and you ask yourself a simple question- "Wouldn't it be interesting, if...?"

That's it. That's all you have to do. Think of what would be interesting or fun to have happen, and then do that, and if you do it well, the audience will love your own new take on something they already adore. If you don't do it well, you'll learn it didn't work and why, and you won't make that mistake again, but it will still improve you as a writer.

So, don't fall into the originality trap- the stories you write aren't going to be original, and your audience doesn't want them to be. What they do want from you is to show them old stories with new eyes, and if you can do that, your work will be seen as fresh and original, even if it really isn't.

GENRE

Once upon a time, stories didn't have genres, and nobody thought in terms of horror, comedy, romance, or action- they just thought in terms of "story." A story was something people told for education, entertainment, and money, so people thought about the actual content of the stories in only the simplest of terms. ("It's the one with the bear." Or perhaps, "The one with the funny bits.") Eventually, however, storytellers learned what worked and what didn't, and audiences learned what they liked and didn't like, and slowly over time certain types of stories appeared, and someone French called these "genres."

Think of a genre as a template or pre-set collection of ideas about what a story should be, and you'll have the right idea. For example, when I mentioned "horror" above, you might have had a flashback to a scary movie on TV you saw when you snuck downstairs after bedtime as a child. Maybe you pictured a man in a mask chasing teenagers or an army of shambling zombies. Anyone who has seen a horror movie knows what they're like, and what to expect, and they also know the "rules" that are associated with a horror movie. It's not hard to understand, because the most basic rule is right there in the name- they're there to make the audience feel "horror" or intense fear.

And every genre is like that, it's a set of goals and expectations, for example:

- Action: The audience wants to watch a skilled fighter beat up villains in a cool manner and do the things that the audience only wishes they could do.
- Comedy: The audience wants to see likeable characters go through hard times but find humor in their situations and come out okay in the end.
- Drama: The audience wants to see human beings facing the problems of being human and dealing with the hard facts of life, and other people, in a way which makes the audience's own problems feel much smaller.
- Romance: The audience wants to confirm their belief that true love wins over the hard realities of life, and see beautiful people find their soulmates.
- Slice of Life: The audience wants to see life from a slightly different perspective that shows them we're all the same at heart, and life can be as funny as it is difficult.
- Superhero: The audience wants the thrills of watching someone greater than human defeat evil in a spectacular manner, and restore a feeling that there is justice in the world.

And so on.

This is great for you as a writer, because it means that when you pick a genre, a big part of your work is already done for you! You already know what your audience wants, and you know the controlling ideas that come with that genre, so all you need to do is start to play with them and add your own original spin to what you already know needs to be there.

However, on the flipside, this is also bad for you as a writer because audiences who want genre stories also know what they want from them, and if you don't give them what they expect, they're not going to be happy. This is why it's important to make sure that when you pick your story's genre it's one you're familiar with, or are willing to spend a lot of time learning about. A fact especially true because genres have what are called "subgenres", and those genres within genres have their own special sets of rules that go with them as well. (A Zombie Horror movie, for example, is very different from a Slasher Horror film, just as a Romantic Comedy is different from a Historical Romance.)

That doesn't mean you can't put your own take on genres, or even mix genres, but what it does mean is that you need to know what the special core ideas of your genre and subgenre. You need to know what the audience demands in a story from that genre, and you need to know what you can leave out or play with. Audiences are pretty forgiving, but if a comedy has no laughs, or a romance has no happy ending, people are going to want their money back. (Or at least leave bad reviews.)

Not that you need to re-invent the wheel- the internet is filled with information about different genres and what their key ideas are. You just need to do your homework before you try writing in areas you're not familiar with.

One final note- As you do research on genres online, you will find lots of lists about "clichés we hate" regarding different genres, and it will be really tempting to make a point of avoiding those clichés in your own work. Be really careful when you do this, because the clichés that some people hate in different genres are the very things that other people love about them, and sometimes the haters actually love them too, they're just complaining because... it's the internet, people do that. This is why it's so important to know your writing genre and decide for yourself what you like and don't like about it, so you can make those choices for yourself.

You'll never make everyone happy anyways, so don't even try.

Write the stories you want to write.

THEME

While an interesting main plot or idea for the story is going to make it interesting to read, the truth is if you want your story to really have any depth, or be meaningful to readers, you're going to need to find a theme for it as well. The theme, as your English teacher probably told your class more than once, is the message or lesson about life that the author is trying to communicate to the reader. It's often the "point" of the story, and works hand in hand with the other controlling ideas to guide the story toward a natural ending. This is another area where you are customizing a story and making it your own, and it is an important one which shouldn't be skipped lightly.

As your teacher might also have taught you, there are two parts to theme: Thematic Idea and Thematic Statement (also sometimes called an Argument). Simply put, the Thematic Idea is the general theme of the story (War, Love, Greed, etc.) and the Thematic Statement is the actual point the writer is trying to make about the Thematic Idea. (War is bad, Love is bittersweet, Greed drives civilization, etc.)

Your job, then, is to match your controlling ideas up with a Thematic Statement that will bring out the best in your story and characters while reflecting your own ideas.

So, first, look at your controlling ideas again and think about possible themes they naturally suggest. If you can't think of any, then take a look at a list of common themes and see if any of them will fit the story you're trying to tell.

For example, let's look at a Core Premise (see Storytelling Weapons and Tactics) for a story:

A mousy college student working in a used bookstore must find a mysterious book when her co-workers are possessed by evil spirits that will escape the store at nightfall.

What are the possible themes that could work with this story?

- Finding confidence in yourself.
- The power of love.
- Not giving up.
- The power of knowledge.
- Revenge.
- The power of friendship.
- Sins of the past returning.

Now, a story can have more than one theme, but it really should only have one main theme (thematic statement), which is the one that truly drives the story forward. This is the lesson the writer is trying to teach the reader, and it will have an enormous influence on both the beginning of the story and its ending. This is why, in many stories, the main character will start the story with their life in a bad place because they haven't accepted the truth which is behind theme of the story.

For example, if the main theme of the above story is "you need to have confidence to succeed," then the main character will start the story with no confidence and her life will be hard because of it. If the story is about "love conquers all," then the main character's secret love for her co-worker will be making her miserable and causing problems in her life and relationships. Or, if the story is about "the sins of the past", the bookstore will be a gloomy place with few customers because a strange dark feeling hangs over the place which is preventing the people there from being truly happy.

Then, you can use the theme of a story to tell you how it should end, because the end of the story must be one which reinforces that theme or idea and proves it's the correct answer. This gives the audience the lesson the writer is trying to prove, and that only by accepting that "truth" can the main character solve the problem established in the beginning and find a happy new life.

For example, if the main theme of the story is "you need to have confidence to succeed," then it will be about a character who is forced to find confidence to save the day and win. If the story is about "love conquers all," then the ending will be about how the main character's secret love for her co-worker is the key to defeating the evil spirits and her confession solves the problem (and her own life issues). Or, if the story is about the "sins of the past," then the story might play out as a mystery where the main character needs to learn whose misdeeds caused this situation and how to remedy them in the present- doing so will stop the curse and leave the bookstore a happier place.

Thus, as you can see, the theme of a story can have a strong influence over its plot, setting, characters, presentation, tone and so much more. In fact, it should be carefully considered because it is often the glue which holds the story together. But, if you find yourself getting stuck on trying to come up with a theme (a common problem for new writers) then the most likely reason is that you're making your life harder than you need to. Most genres (and subgenres) have traditional themes that are already attached to them, and all you need to do is go look carefully back at the themes of some of your favorite stories to find one which one interests you or moves you. Then, if you want to be a little different, try making a small twist on that usual theme.

For example, in a Romance story, a common theme is "A woman needs a strong man, and a man needs a smart woman." But, you might take that theme and play with it, making it into something like, "A man needs a strong woman, and a woman needs a smart man." This could produce a different story than the usual, and could provide the audience with something they don't see very often.

The truth is, there is no one way to pick your story's theme, but here are a few suggestions which might help.

- Pick a topic which you are passionate about, decide what your position is on it, and then develop the story accordingly. Write.
- Pick a topic you know others are passionate about and will buy stories about, and plan a story around a theme and argument they will like. Write.
- Pick a theme from a list online, then decide what your position is on that theme and either plan your story with this in mind, or write your story with this in mind, and revise accordingly.
- Create a lead character, figure out what themes this character would be best to explore, and then pick one and take a position on it. Plan and write.

- Figure out what the common theme and argument of the type of story you like is, then use that theme to write your own stories using that theme and argument. (This will also make it appeal to the people who love this theme like you do.)
- Figure out what the common theme and argument of the type of story you like is, then reverse that theme to write your own stories using the opposite of that argument. (This can sometimes produce "genre busting" or "deconstructionist" works which will get people's attention, like George R.R. Martin's *A Song of Ice and Fire* (aka *A Game of Thrones*) or the Western movie *Unforgiven*.)
- Pick your theme (or don't), write the story without knowing what your point is, then go back and find it hidden (or not so hidden) in there. Once you know what the theme is, revise the story, characters and setting to fit that theme. (This is a favorite method of those who enjoy writing without a clear plan.)

The important part is taking a general thematic idea (like friendship, peace, revenge) and then turning it into a clear thematic statement which gives your story a direction and goal. Just leaving it as a general idea is asking for trouble and a lot of rewriting down the line as you try to find a theme from a direction-less story.

ENGAGEMENT

When you are writing, there are two main ways you can make a story engaging to readers- interest and conflict.

Stories driven by interest keep the reader's attention by presenting the story in a fascinating way. For example, providing information, situations, or events which the reader finds appealing, and keeps their focus on the story because they want more of what the writer is giving them.

On the other hand, stories driven by conflict are stories where the reader is kept involved in the story by their desire to see the character overcome challenges as they try to accomplish their goals. Whether the conflict is direct (as in two people battling each other) or indirect (as in a character trying to get a good score on a math test) the core of the story is the character and the obstacles they face as they struggle to achieve their ambitions.

Naturally, most stories include elements of both of these. It's rare to find a story where a character doesn't have at least some challenges to face in accomplishing their aims, and any good storyteller layers their tales with information and events which the audience is going to find engaging. However, these two things are separate approaches, and you can tell interesting stories with little conflict, or conflict-driven stories which stick to the bare bones and are just about the characters and their challenging objectives.

To better understand each, let's look at them in more detail.

Interest-Driven Stories

At one end of the spectrum are interest-driven stories: stories which are engaging because they present the audience with things that the audience finds interesting or appealing. The human brain doesn't just love information that comes from conflict and things going right or wrong, it also loves to be given emotional stimulation and information that it considers useful for our survival. You can even tell whole stories where the audience is carried along by the love of the experiences that the story is giving them, rather than any central conflict. In fact, it's possible to tell a story without any conflict at all, but still make it fun and interesting to the audience.

The ways to keep an audience engaged using their interest can generally be broken down into two categories- what you give and what you withhold.

Let's look at each.

What you Give Your Audience

There are generally five things that stories can give their audiences to make them interested, and all stories provide some of these directly or indirectly. The simplest way to remember them is to use the acronym SPICE, which represents the five key things audiences get from stories- Skills, Perspective, Information, Creativity, and Emotion.

Skills – If a story teaches the audience how to do something, whether it's growing plants, judging wine, star-ship tactical combat, solving crossword puzzles, or how to get a good night's sleep, then the audience will consider that story interesting. Many otherwise dull or cliché stories have been given new life by having the character (and thus the audience) acquire a new skill as a part of the story, and thus become an enjoyable learning experience.

Perspective – If a story offers a new way of seeing the world, or on the other hand, confirms or supports the way the audience already sees the world, then they will likely consider it interesting. In our lives, we only really know our own points of view, and stories let us see the world as others see it- that's one of the wonderful parts about experiencing a story. On the flipside, we naturally want our own views of the world to be the correct ones, and stories that back up and support those views will resonate with an audience that wants those views to be true. This might sound sinister to some, but most popular stories have a version of this buried inside them which acts as a comfort to the audience – "good will always triumph over evil", "if you work hard you will succeed in life", "there's someone out there for everyone", "there's justice in this world", etc.

Information – If a story offers the audience knowledge about a subject they're not familiar with, they will consider it interesting. This is different from Skills in that it isn't teaching the audience how to do something, but giving them information about a topic or topics. This can be history, culture, fashion, philosophy, sports, nature, geophysics, religion, and everything in between. If the audience is interested in this topic, or made to be interested in it by the presentation of the story, then they'll stick with it. Audiences remember the plots and conflicts of great fiction, but those books were often also filled with information about the world as well which subtly helped to make them the classics they are.

Creativity – If the story offers the audience something new, or that they haven't seen before, they will consider it interesting. This can be any aspect of the story from how it makes them feel, to the way it's told (character, plot, setting, style, structure, etc.) to the content (skills, perspective, information) that is new to the audience. Give them something they don't know, they haven't seen done, or they haven't seen done this way, and you'll have earned a lot of interest in the work. (But never sacrifice quality for novelty- novelty might carry a short story, but it will rarely carry an entire book by itself.)

Emotion – If a story can make the audience feel something, then they will find it interesting. (Although not always enjoyable.) All good stories should make the audience feel something at some point, and certain kinds of stories are even built around producing specific kinds of emotion. (Horror, Romance, Erotica, Comedy, Tragedy, etc.) If you can elicit emotions from your audience, and it's the emotions they want to feel, then they'll stay with you to enjoy the emotional ride.

Not every story will contain all five of these things, nor all five things in the same ratios, but if you want your audience to think of a story as being "good" you'll probably want to think about which ones your story is offering and in what ways. Obviously, not all stories teach the audience how to do something, but most do offer some new information. Similarly, not every audience wants creativity, or at least a lot of it, as sometimes a familiar story gives them comfort and new things can sometimes be challenging.

The key is that the more you're aware of these elements, and how you're using them, the better your story can be because you can control and shape them to get the results you want as opposed to just guessing how to satisfy your audience. These five elements should be thought of as being like spices in cooking, and using them properly can turn a bland story into a tasty meal for the audience. And not just a story, scenes and even dialog can be brought to life by thinking about how to add these small elements to paint a greater picture.

What you Withhold from your Audience

What happens next?

This is a question that your audience should always be asking, and always be wanting to know the answer to. If they don't want to know, or don't care, your story is dull, or possibly even worse- dead.

The above question, and ones like it, are called Dramatic Questions, and they're the hidden power of your story which keeps your audience glued to the story to the point where they will ignore everything, even food or sleep, to find out the answers to the questions you've created inside their minds. They're the hidden seasoning that makes a plain story into a gripping one, and a simple story into something that you can't put down.

So, how do you work this magic?

Well, there's an old saying about the ancient Chinese board game *Go*: "Easy to learn, a lifetime to master." This saying applies equally to dramatic questions, because while the concept is simple, learning to master their power can span a writer's whole career.

So, here's the easy part.

To create dramatic questions all a writer needs to do is to introduce a situation or problem, and then not tell the audience the result or answer until later in the most dramatic or interesting way possible.

As mentioned before, all stories are actually mysteries- at the beginning of the story the audience is given a situation that creates what is called the Major Dramatic Question (this is the one which lasts the whole story) and then the audience spends the story trying to figure out how the Major Dramatic Question will resolve. Along the way, there are also many smaller dramatic questions in each scene and chapter which keep the story moving towards an ending where all (or most) of the questions will be answered to the audience's satisfaction.

This actually sounds more complicated than it is, so let's break it down further.

Somewhere near the beginning of a story, the audience is introduced to a character with a goal, and often that goal has a natural question that comes with it- "will the character succeed?" This is a "yes or no" question which will take the whole story to answer, and when the question is answered the story is finished, which is why we call it the Major Dramatic Question.

This should be a simple and primal question that anyone can understand, based around actions like winning, saving, finding, getting or escaping. Will Bob win the golf tournament? Does Colleen save her friend? Does Lin reach the market in time? Does Ali find his lost love? Can Sue escape the King's guard? These are all dramatic questions based on actions and goals any audience member can recognize and ones people will find interesting and want to know the answers to.

However, keeping them reading requires a whole other set of dramatic questions. Because, unless you are writing short flash fiction which only has time for a single dramatic question, you're going to need to create a long series of other smaller dramatic questions to keep the story interesting and moving forward. Stories are built on two forces- uncertainty and curiosity, and the best writing produces a constant uncertainty in the audience about what will happen next while making the audience want to know the answers to questions you introduce.

Again, it sounds complicated, but is fundamentally simple. Everything you introduce into the story has a dramatic question that comes with it (how will this affect the story/situation/character's lives?) and the audience is already looking for those story elements which produce those questions. You just need to introduce interesting things and let the audience's own curiosity and imagination about the kinds of events those things will produce carry the story along and keep them reading.

For example:

- Bob and Sue want to get married. (Characters + Goal = Major Dramatic Question = Will they get married? Yes or No?)
- But Bob is a gambler who owes gangsters money. (Who are these gangsters? What will they do if he doesn't pay? How much does he owe? Will this affect their relationship?)
- Bob is afraid to tell Sue the truth. (Will he do it? Why? How will it affect their relationship and marriage plans if he does?)
- Sue snoops and reads Bob's phone messages. (What will happen now that she knows the truth? How will Bob feel about her snooping?)
- Sue confronts Bob, they fight and break up. (Is the marriage off?)

- In front of Sue, Bob is taken by gangsters who want their money. (What will happen to Bob?)
- Sue calls the police. (How will this affect the situation? Will this help or make things worse?)
- And so on.

As you can see, the simple "Bob and Sue want to get married" premise is the foundation of the story, and creates a central question which will be answered by the end of the story. Each new Event or story element which introduced then creates more and more questions the reader must read to find out the answers to, and while some questions are answered, others are constantly being created to keep the story interesting and carry the reader from one point to the next.

Key points where you want to introduce questions are at the beginning of scenes (what will happen in the scene? How will it turn out?) and at the ends of scenes (often by leaving some part of the scene unresolved) and similarly at the beginning and end of chapters. A very common pattern in stories is that no scene (except at the end) ever completely answers a question and the audience must wait until another scene to find out how things turned out. By doing this, the writer keeps the audience in a constant state of wondering what will happen, or how things turned out, until the very end.

As you can see, this is a simple concept which requires a bit of skill to use properly. If you're a beginning writer, don't get too worked up about all this and just focus on three things:

1. Make sure your story has a Major Dramatic Question you clearly lay out to the audience as soon as you can at the start of the story and don't answer until the end.
2. Make sure each scene generates at least one question the audience will want answered later.
3. Make sure each chapter (or sequence) ends on a big question that will make the audience want to keep going to find out the answer to.

And naturally, if you're going to make the audience ask questions, make sure that you do answer them. Audiences that are left with major unanswered questions write bad reviews, unless you make it very clear that those questions are going to be answered in the next part of the story.

Working as a Team

Together, by giving your audience what they enjoy, and making your audience ask questions- you keep them engaged and interested in your story. Even with little to no actual conflict, it's possible to tell a story that audiences will want to binge because they're enjoying it so much. A perfect example of this is the genre known as Slice of Life, which is a whole genre built around characters living their mundane daily lives, but which is popular because Slice of Life writers know how to keep their audiences happy through interesting material (SPICE) and introducing dramatic questions that their audiences want to know the answer to.

Conflict-Driven Stories

Human brains love stories because they can learn from them, and while there are things to be learned from stories about everything going right, there's a lot more to be learned from stories about things going wrong. We're drawn to stories about characters facing challenges- we want to know how others deal with adversity and overcome it. It's the same impulse that has you rubbernecking at a car accident or drinking in the latest criminal events in the news- we want to know when and how things go wrong (so we can avoid them).

As mentioned above, conflict comes in two flavors- direct and indirect. Direct conflict is when two or more characters are actively trying to work against each other, usually because they're after the same (or similar) goal. This can range from two swordsmen dueling, to a love triangle, or even a sleuth trying to uncover a criminal - there is a prize that everyone wants and few can have (even if it's just the truth), and they're all actively working in their own ways to get it. Most stories are built around direct conflict because it's both easier to write and more engaging for readers. Plus, it makes things more personal because you can put a face to both sides and know their motivations and desires.

Indirect conflict, on the other hand, is when there is no clear person or group actively working against the main character and their goals. There may be characters who stand between the main character and their finish line, but they're not actively trying to stop the main character from achieving whatever their goals are. Maybe the character is running a marathon, or maybe they're just trying to get their work done in time to leave when the clock hits five. Either way, the character has things they need to accomplish which are challenging in some way, but nobody is aggressively trying to stop them. In your own life, you spend most of your time in indirect conflicts with the world around you in one way or another – getting to work on time, finishing homework to meet deadlines, trying to measure up to parental expectations. Direct conflict is actually rare in the real world, but indirect conflict is everywhere- maybe that's why we find direct conflict so fascinating.

There are four other factors that also affect how interesting the conflict is in stories- emotional connection, intensity, stakes, and level of challenge. Each of them is a different element writers can play with to determine how engaging the conflict is and how the audience will perceive it.

The most basic thing that determines how engaging a conflict will be for the audience will be how much they like (or at least connect) with the characters involved. The more emotionally connected they are to the characters, the more intensely the audience will experience the conflict because they have strong feelings about the main characters and want to see them succeed or fail in their goals. The chapter on Audience goes into great detail about how to accomplish this connection, but it's a factor in conflict that should never be ignored. An audience's emotional connection to a character (even if they want to see them get beaten to a pulp) will determine a lot about their interest in the outcome of any conflict.

The next factor is Intensity, which refers to how focused the story is on the central conflict(s) of the story. For example, a boxing match is a very intense situation where every move and every blow can make the difference between victory and defeat. This kind of intense situation can make for exciting storytelling, and keeps the audience on the edge of their seats to see what will happen next because everything they're seeing is important to the characters and the results of the story. On the other hand, we can also have low-intensity conflict, like when two managers at a company are dueling for an upcoming promotion by both working hard to impress their bosses. This conflict might play out over days, week, or even months, and while it's happening other things are going on as well. Not everything they do will affect the outcome, and the intensity of this conflict is very low.

In theory, any kind of conflict-based story, direct or indirect, can be presented with any kind of intensity. The boxing match could be made low intensity by mixing their actions with lots of flashbacks and jumps to side stories and side characters. A match is happening, but it's being purposely slowed down to present it in a slower paced and deliberate way. On the other hand, the dueling office managers conflict could be made extremely intense if the story focuses just on what actions they take which move them closer or further away from their goals, and ignores most of the other things happening in their lives. It's all about how much focus you put on the conflict itself.

Another major factor that affects how conflict plays out in stories is stakes- what the character is risking as they try to accomplish their goals. Or, to put it another way- what price will they pay if they fail? The bigger the price they will pay, the more attention-grabbing the conflict becomes, and the more the audience will want to see if the character succeeds. (At least, if the audience cares about the character or their goals.) Watching someone gamble their lunch money in a game of poker is mildly interesting, but watching someone risk their house, car and life savings on a throw of the dice in Vegas is mesmerizing.

Undeniably, the biggest set of stakes that most characters can risk in a story is death, and there are some who say that unless a character is risking death of some kind then a story isn't worth telling. While this is going a little too far (you can tell a perfectly good story where the stakes are a ham sandwich), there's no doubt that the biggest thrills come from watching a character risk their life to try and make their dreams happen. And, that death can come in many forms, for while we usually think of death in the physical sense, characters can die psychologically and socially as well. A ruined career is still a form of death if a character has built their life around their work, and social death is something that even a child in kindergarten can experience.

The end of your world as you know it is death- no matter what form it takes.

The final element to think about when trying to create dramatic conflict is the level of challenge the character(s) have to face. How difficult is it going to be to accomplish their goals? The more difficult the task, the more interesting it is to the audience, because the audience loves to see how characters overcome challenges that look hard or even impossible. Just putting the character in a situation where the audience can't see the solution creates an immediate huge dramatic question- how will they overcome this? And, it's a question that's so powerful that it drives entire stories, and keeps audiences guessing, wondering and interested in the conflict.

Together, emotional connections, intensity, stakes, and challenge are what help make a conflict interesting to an audience, and every conflict must have all of these at some level. A low-intensity/low-stakes story like two children on a field trip trying to find the best fossils still has elements of intensity and stakes that writers can play with, while a high-intensity/high-stakes situation like a battle in an arena pit with a mother defending her child against a dragon is about as gripping as you can get. However, nothing says that the intensity and stakes have to be high or low, and you can turn the story about the girl risking her lunch money in noontime poker into spellbinding drama by ramping up the intensity of what is otherwise a low-stakes situation. Similarly, if those two kids collecting fossils are unknowingly doing something that will result in one of them dying if they fail, you've turned a normal low-intensity day into a horrific nail-biting situation for the audience.

A likeable character facing a large challenge will get the audience attention's every time, and if there's serious stakes involved, and the story has at least some medium level of intensity, then that's a recipe for a thrilling ride that no reader wants to miss.

A many trying to help his brother- *mildly interesting.* (emotional connection)

A man trying to help his brother climb a castle wall- *interesting.* (emotion + challenge)

A man and his brother who have thirty seconds to climb a castle wall- *really interesting.* (emotion + challenge + intensity)

A man who has thirty seconds to climb a castle wall or his brother will die- *you can't look away.* (emotion + challenge + intensity + stakes = winner!)

Interest versus Conflict?

It might be tempting to think of Interest and Conflict as being opposites, like they're two ends of a spectrum, but the reality is that they're both just ways to get your audience to become interested and involved in your story. You can have a high conflict story which is also filled with extremely interesting details and question hooks, and you can have an interest-driven story with periods of high tension and conflict- they're not mutually exclusive. The better way of think of them is as different elements that writers can play with when they write.

But do remember, the more interesting details a story is filled with, the slower it will tend to become, so if you're planning to write a gripping action-thriller, stuffing it full of interesting information about a city or advanced trigonometry might not be the best of ideas. It's all about including only the relevant details that are connected with the story and finding a balance between being interesting and being exciting that works for you and your audience.

FINAL TIP

Everything in this section (and in fact this book) is a collection of things to think about, and if something doesn't work for you then you should ignore it. While theme, dramatic questions, genres and engagement are all things writers often think of when planning a story, consciously or unconsciously, if you find thinking about them gets in the way then don't feel you have to spend too much time on them.

On the other hand, these are some of the important controlling ideas which help to shape stories, and so you need to be aware of them. The more you think about them, and the more you use their power, the better you will find your stories become. Writing is as much a science as it is an art, and much of what you've read in this chapter is wisdom that has been passed down and learned by writers that have come before you.

Use their learning to help kickstart your own writing, and to make yourself a better writer. Just as we don't need to re-invent fire or the wheel each generation, you don't need to re-invent writing, and the faster you become a writer, and a good one, the faster the world of fiction becomes a better place.

CHARACTER

There are many who think that all there is to characters is creating an interesting main character they're passionate about and everything else will fall into place. Sometimes that is true, and for some writers all they need is for that amazing lead character to ignite the fires of their creativity and then write volumes of work.

However, in most cases, just having a cool and interesting lead character isn't enough.

It must be the right cool and interesting main character for the project. One who reflects the story's themes and ideals, one who is a natural part of the setting they inhabit, and one who is at the center of a network of other characters who act as funhouse mirrors of the main character or the story's central point. Unless that main character fits into the project perfectly, and reflects the goals of the story they're a part of, they can be amazing in the writer's imagination, but will ultimately fall flat in the minds of the readers the writer needs to persuade.

It's only by knowing how characters come together with the story and setting that characters really come to life, and a writer must be able to craft characters which represent both the story and themselves onto the page and into the minds of the audience.

So, how should you go about creating great characters?

The truth is, there is no set way to create characters for stories. How characters are created will depend largely on the writer and the role the characters need to play, but there are a few best practices.

BUILDING CHARACTERS

The two basic ways to create characters are top-down and bottom-up.

Let's talk about the top-down method first, because it's the simpler of the two. In the top-down method you take an archetype (a common type of person or social role, like cop, doctor, smarmy used car salesman, or friendly grandmother) which the audience knows well, and then you customize that character as needed for their role in the story. You make them look slightly different, sound different, or act different, but at heart they're still based on an archetype.

This is especially useful for minor characters and background characters, who don't need to really be all that unique, and are mostly there to just say their lines and go. However, there is nothing that says that you can't make all of your characters this way, especially if you're a beginning writer who finds it easier to work with established ideas. Top-down characters are as much roles as they are people, and they're ones the audience likely knows well, so they're perfect for quick, short jobs when you don't need a lot of depth or detail. (Although you can give them as much depth and detail as you want.)

The opposite is bottom-up designed characters, which as you might be able to guess are characters that are designed completely yourself. You create a set of attributes or ideas, and then slowly develop them out to create a character who is special and unique. You might make fifty pages of notes about the character and know every last detail about them, or you might just know the minimum you need to write them in your story, but either way they're completely yours and unique reflections of your worldview.

Again, there are no set rules for making bottom-up characters, but there are a few things that you should probably know about them. First, you should know their general description and how they dress. Second, they should always have a need or goal of some kind, which will be what motivates them and drives them. Third, they should have some features which make them unique compared to the world around them on each level (internally like how they view the world, and externally like how they dress or act, for example). And last, fourth, you should know the role(s) they're going to play in the story and what functions they'll fill.

CHARACTER ROLES

In terms of story structure, there are four kinds of characters.

- Main Characters
- Opponents
- Support Characters
- Background Characters

Each of these has their place and each fills a different role in stories. And this is very important to remember- characters in stories are not real people. They might sound real, act real, or even feel real to the reader, but like everything else in a story, they are a creation of the writer which is there to serve the needs of the story. Similarly, they don't exist on their own, but in relation to the story and setting around them.

So, for example, Hannah Tachibana (mentioned in the Plot chapter), the aspiring sushi chef, is a main character who exists to represent the ideal of trying hard in life and succeeding through effort. She is female because the story is about entering a world usually dominated by men, and half-Japanese because this makes her an outsider finding her place in Japanese culture, both of which serve to make the reader sympathetic towards her while at the same time creating interest, drama, and story opportunities. She will be defined by her actions and her interactions with the people around her (mentor, friends, opponents, etc.), and through them we will learn about who she is.

In a story about a young foreigner trying to become a sushi chef in Japan, she's perfect for the role, and fits nicely. However, if we take Hannah and place her in a story about international spies, or on a superhero drama, she will likely be totally out of place, or become a different character than she would be in a story about her rise in the Japanese food industry. She will also change the story that she's in, as the writer attempts to fit Hannah into that story in a relevant way and connect her to the main ideas and themes of the story. Story and setting shape the character, and the character shapes the setting and story in a symbiotic relationship.

Likewise, the other characters around Hannah will be reflections of her, and we will learn about them by being compared with Hannah. Through Hannah's work ethic, we see how the other students in her cooking school measure up. Through Hannah's philosophy of cooking, we see how they view the relationship between people and food. And similarly, through the reflected actions of Hannah's opponents, we learn about what kind of person Hannah is and her strengths and weaknesses.

"No man is an island," wrote poet John Donne, and this is doubly true for fictional characters.

Now, with that in mind, let's look at those four types of characters and the roles they fill.

MAIN CHARACTERS

The lead character in a story is there as the reader's guide. They are there to take the audience on a journey through the story, and give the audience a perspective on whatever the story's point or argument is. Their experiences will be the heart of the story, and their trip through that story will be what makes the reader love it or hate it.

There is great debate over whether main characters need to be likeable. Some, like writer Blake Snyder of *Save the Cat!* fame, take the position that making a connection between the audience and the lead character is crucial to a successful story. Others take a different view, and say that bonding with the lead character is optional, but that finding the main character interesting is the key. However, both sides still agree that the main character is the most important link between the audience and the story- one that will make or break your story.

Also, writers must understand the difference between the main character and the protagonist. The main character is the audience's window to the world the character lives in, while the protagonist is a person whose goals and desires drive the story and make the events happen. Usually, these are the same person, and so this book just uses the terms "main character" and "lead" interchangeably, however you should know that this isn't always the case. Some stories separate the main character and the protagonist into two people, the classic example being Sherlock Holmes and Doctor Watson. Holmes is the protagonist, but Watson is the main character who tells us about Holmes and the amazing adventures his friend has.

In any case, one of the better descriptions of the attributes of a good main character comes from the Greek philosopher Aristotle and his book on playwriting *Poetics*, where he says that the central character in a story should have the following attributes:

1. They should be a <u>good person</u>, as audiences won't bond or connect with those they see as villains. (Or at least, they should have some positive qualities that the audience agrees with.)

2. They should be <u>acceptable</u>, as audiences must believe characters are people who would have the traits they do. (No 15-year-old MBAs, or 21-year-old military generals unless it can be well explained. The character must be believable within their setting.)

3. They should be <u>consistent</u>, as audiences want main characters they understand, and ones who don't change too much or too quickly. (This means that

once you say a character is a certain way (smart, dumb, brave, cowardly, etc.) then you have to stick with that, or have a good reason for the change.)

4. They should be consistently inconsistent, as audiences don't like to be confused by the main character, so the writer better be ready to explain the reasons why when the character breaks their usual patterns in some way. (As in #3, having a good reason why don't follow the usual patterns of behavior for the character.)

So, to sum up, Aristotle felt a good main character is one who has at least some relatable positive attributes to allow for good audience connection, was believable, stable in who they are, and understandable in their occasional shifts or changes of direction. Which, if you think about, sums up not only the attributes of a good character, but also a good story as well! Not bad for 335 BCE!

On top of that, there is one more attribute that a good main character should probably have, and that is they should want something. After all, a main character who meets all of the above requirements can still be boring as toast if they just sit there and don't do anything.

Goals

Just like successful people, successful lead characters have goals or things they want to accomplish. The character needs a reason to take action, and they will either be Active Leads (who choose to take action to accomplish a goal), or Passive Leads (someone or something else forces them to take action).

The Active Lead is a character who drives the story with their actions. They have a clear goal (Rebuild the Kingdom, Win the Love of the Billionaire, solve the crime, etc) and everything they do in the story is about working forward towards that goal. They take actions, those actions have consequences, and the character dealing with the consequences of those actions is what makes up a lot of the story. The rest of the cast is there to support the Active Lead, and has usually been chosen by them to help accomplish their goal. However, the supporting cast could all die off and the story would still continue because the Active Lead would still keep trying to achieve their goal. (And, likely now do it to live up to the dreams of the people who fell in their noble quest.)

The Passive Lead, on the other hand, is a character is a character who has little to no idea of what their goals are and is just reacting to situations and circumstances as they come. Usually the Passive Lead is just trying to muddle through their life, has no great aspirations, and if they were given a choice would probably rather be at home in their room playing video games. However, usually because other characters have become part of their lives, and they do have some basic sense of responsibility or duty, they become involved in the story and participate in the events that happen. Often, they do want to do something more with their lives, but are afraid to try or don't know how, and will slowly find their way thanks to the other more active characters who become part of their new world.

It will come as no surprise that active characters are almost always better, since the audience can learn more from a character who is trying to actively accomplish a goal, and they're easier to write. However, whether they're active or passive, character goals still generally fall into one of three simple categories:

- Attain
- Maintain
- Lose

The character either wants something they don't have (attain), they want to avoid losing something that already exists (maintain), or they no longer wish to have something and try to get rid of it (lose). All characters will have one of these three goals, with the details varying by the scene and story, and by keeping the goals simple and primal like this, it makes them easier to write and easier for the audience to relate to, which is always important.

Now, why are they pursuing that goal?

That comes down to the other important thing a writer should know about their character- what's their motivation?

Motivations

In addition to the character having a goal, the audience also wants to know why the character is working towards that goal. What's the character's reasons for doing what they do?

Here's just a few things establishing a character's motivation does:

- It sets up the direction and focus of the story.
- It helps the reader understand why the character does what they do.
- It can make the reader empathize with the character.
- It can make the reader interested in seeing how the character accomplishes the goal and how it turns out.

These are all important things, so planning a character's motivation should never be overlooked as part of your story. Some writers prefer to make it a bit of a mystery because they know the audience wants to know this information, and that's fine, just so long as you, the writer, know what it is from the start.

Here is a brief list of a few common motivations that drive characters:

- Acceptance (the character wants to be accepted by others)
- Accomplishment (the character wants to achieve a particular goal or a sense of having done something worthwhile)
- Boredom (the character is easily bored and wants something interesting to do)
- Challenge (the character desires to test their skills or abilities against others)
- Compassion (the character wants to help others fill their needs)
- Curiosity (the character wants to learn more about something)
- Fame (the character wants their name to known by others)
- Family (the character is driven by their love of their family members or the idea of family)
- Fear (the character is driven to avoid something or someone)
- Fighting (the character enjoys physical or verbal conflict)
- Food (the character desires food or eating experiences)
- Friendship (the character wants to gain or maintain close friendships)
- Greed (the character wants to acquire something)
- Guilt (the character is trying to make up for some past misdeeds, real or perceived)
- Honor (the character wants to uphold values held by their clan, group or society)
- Ideology (the character has a strong belief in an idea or system (like religion, or a code of conduct) that motivates what they do)
- Independence (the character is driven by a need for personal freedom)
- Knowledge (the character wants to gain information, skills or an experience)
- Love/Hate (the character loves/hates someone or something)
- Novelty (the character wants to have new experiences)
- Order (the character wants to create order in their life or environment)
- Physical Activity (the character wants to exercise their body)
- Power (the character wants control over others and the things that come with it)
- Responsibility (the character feels responsibility towards someone or something)
- Revenge (the character feels they been harmed or wronged, and wants to return the favor)

- Safety (the character wants to feel secure and protected)
- Savings (the character wants to accumulate something)
- Sex (the character wants to have sex with others)
- Social Status (the character wants to increase their status in society)
- Survival (the character wants to get the things they need to live)

Of course, this is hardly a complete list (these are all very generic) and they also need to be developed more to go with a particular character in a particular story, but they're a start, and they let us use a simple formula to figure out why characters are doing what they do:

The character will attain/maintain/lose X if they (do or not do) Y.

X is a motivating reason, and Y is an action or state.

For example:

- The character will attain money if they do a job.
- The character will maintain their honor if they get revenge on their enemy.
- The character will lose social status if they fail to attend the ball.
- The character will attain love if they find the right romantic partner.

Simple, right? By doing it this way, we can easily understand any character's motivations and the reasons they're driven to try to achieve their goals they are. Whether they're Story Motivations or Core Motivations.

To get the simplest one out of the way first, Story Motivations are the reasons a character acts the way they do in a particular story or situation. For example, they're hungry so they buy food, or they see a monster so they run away. Story Motivations are usually obvious and clear-cut, because they often come from outside events happening around the character or to the character. They can come from the plot, setting, or even the character themselves, and are what helps to motivate the character in this story. However, most Story Motivations are also short-term, and once the reason for acting or reacting is gone, the character is no longer motivated by them. (Once the character has passed a test, for example, they no longer need to study as hard.)

Story Motivations are what often gets the character taking action in stories, and they let the audience learn about the character through how the character reacts to them, but mostly Story Motivations exist to reveal the true nature of the character-their Core Motivations.

Core Motivations are the strongest driving force behind the character's actions, and they help to define what the character is trying to accomplish in the story.

For example, a predominantly greedy character will do what they do because they're after money, or a predominantly cowardly character will try hard to avoid dangerous or confrontational situations. These are examples of Core Motivations, which are so strong they often help to define who the character actually is.

In addition, it's very common for a character to have more than one Core Motivation at the same time, just as real people often have multiple reasons for doing what they do. Giving characters multiple Core Motivations will make them seem more nuanced and real to the audience, and can provide more story ideas for the writer to work with. (Especially if they have conflicting motivations, because that's another way to generate story ideas!)

For example, how would a character whose primary motivations are Safety and Power reconcile those two potentially conflicting motivations? Likely they'd try to gain power in the safest ways possible, perhaps becoming a civil servant, and then work very hard to both gain more power while also keeping their position solid by eliminating their competition. If you combine this with a talent for talking to people, you end up with a scheming politician!

Generally, try to pick two or three Core Motivations for your main characters, and one or two for your supporting cast. Then develop those motivations in your own notes to explain why the characters have the motivations they do and where they came from. Figuring out the source of their motivations will often produce the history of a character better than most character development techniques because it will tell you the defining moments and influences in the character's background that shaped them and made them who they are today.

That said, remember to keep your Core Motivations and their origins simple and straightforward. The audience will need to be able to understand them, or guess them based on how the characters act and behave, and the more relatable the motivations and their origins are, the better the audience can connect with the character. Motivations are often based on basic human needs and desires, and keeping them close to the core desires that all humans have makes them easier to understand for a larger audience.

Lastly, as mentioned at the top, your characters motivations should reflect the ideas or themes you are trying to explore in your story. They should be motivations the character has because those needs will take them in the direction you want them to go, and provide the motivation they need to keep going in that direction until the story reaches its natural ending. (Which is usually when they fill their needs, unless it's tragedy, in which case the needs will be left unfilled in the end because they went about trying to fill them in the wrong way.)

Speaking of character development, how and what the needs of the character are will also depend on whether that character is one of the two types of main characters- Changing, or Unchanging.

Changing Characters

The first type of main character is the Changing character- a character who is actively changing from being one person to being another as the story goes on. Specifically, they are changing internally due to the events which they experience in the course of the story. This is sometimes referred to as the "character's arc," and describes how they change as a person as the story progresses. For example, the character might go from being cowardly to brave, or closed to open, or naïve to experienced. Of course, the change doesn't always have to be positive, either, and it's possible to have characters go from being happy to sad, or romantic to jaded, or caring to hateful. However, if they do have a negative arc, they will usually pull out of it and return to a positive one before the story is over. (Unless it's a tragedy, of course.)

Unchanging Characters

The second type is naturally, a character who doesn't change significantly as the events of the story play out. They might show some small degree of change, but the majority of the things they experience will not change who the character is and they will finish the story largely the same as they entered it. Perhaps they will be a little older, wiser, or more powerful, but any major changes which happen will external to the character (the setting/world around them) and not to the core of who they are. These are characters who change and affect their world, but don't let it change them. They represent ideals, and are often more than human because they are the ones around which their worlds turn. This can make them fascinating people, or this can make them a bit dull unless they are surrounded by other characters who do change, or unless they're doing really interesting things.

Both of these types of main characters are useful, but it's important for writers to know which their leads are right from the beginning. Commonly, if the story a writer is trying to tell is character-driven, then the lead will normally be a changing character, because the character's choices will affect them and make them different as the story goes on. On the other hand, if the story is setting-driven, where the story is about the setting and world the character lives in, normally the lead character will be unchanging. This is because the lead character is most often a window or viewpoint into that setting, and their personal story isn't the point, the setting is. Finally, if the story is plot-driven, then the lead character could be either changing or unchanging, depending on what best suits the type of story the writer is trying to tell.

To give some examples from film, characters like Luke Skywalker, Will Turner, Frodo Baggins, and Harry Potter are all changing characters who start and finish their stories as significantly different people. Meanwhile, Indiana Jones, James

Bond, Doctor Who, and Batman are unchanging characters who are windows to their worlds and don't need to change, nor do audiences want them to.

Unchanging leads were popular in TV and media throughout most of the twentieth century because they're perfect for episodic television. They allow the story to start and finish with a character the audience can get to know, but who never really changes, and the writers never have to worry about where in a character's life or story they are because they're always the same. Audiences actually find these types of characters enjoyable too, because they can offer a comfortable world where nothing really changes and everybody knows their name. (To paraphrase the sitcom Cheers. Sitcoms being another perfect example of unchanging characters in action.)

On the other hand, 21st century audiences have come to love watching changing leads grow and develop in the era of serial television and long form storytelling. Thanks to being able to watch TV series from the beginning whenever they want, audiences now desire progression in the story leads so that they can feel the story is moving somewhere. As novelists have long known, there is a joy to watching a character grow and develop and seeing their triumphs and failures, and it often offers much more for the audience to enjoy than a static hero or heroine who never steps a millimeter outside of their archetype.

Which type of character you make your lead will depend largely on what your goals as a writer are, what your medium is, and what your audience expects. In short, if you want to write a story which will never need to end and has endless storytelling opportunities, then have unchanging leads. On the other hand, if you have a medium where the audience can easily go back and find the beginning, the choice is up to you.

OPPONENTS

An opponent is anyone who that stands in the way of the main character achieving their goals. Frequently, they have the same goal as the main character, and/or have conflicting a worldview or set of values to the main character. There are two basic types of Opponents in stories- those in Active Opposition to the main character and those in Passive Opposition.

Active Opposition– this is an opponent who is actively trying to prevent the main character from achieving their goal. Usually they have the same (or similar) goal as the main character, and this common goal brings them into direct opposition with each other. Often, they also have a superior position to the main character in some way, at least in terms of knowledge, resources, power or ability. (After all, if they weren't able to give the main character a challenge, they're not much of an opponent, are they?) Usually, they are also built specifically to exploit the weaknesses of the main character, thus making them exactly the right person to make the main character's life difficult.

Passive Opposition- an opponent who stands in the way of the character achieving their goals, but who isn't pursuing the same goal as the main character. They are pursuing their own goals, but because of their existence/presence it prevents the main character from achieving their goal. Think of this like a sleeping guard dog that prevents a character from sneaking into the house, the parent who says the main character must clean their room before they can go out, or a clerk at a tax office who says the main character must follow procedure before they can have what they want (as time is running out). Even the character's partners, loved ones, and friends can be passive opponents depending on the situation and circumstances.

Nevertheless, both types have the same jobs- to provide opposition to the Main Character and through that opposition create drama, teach us about the main character, make the main character grow, and represent opposing views to whatever argument or ideals the main character represents. (Usually by presenting the wrong way of doing what the main character is trying to do.)

For example, let's say the story is a serial about a character who wants to be the world's best chef. Naturally, he's going to come in conflict with other chefs on his way to the top, and each of those chefs (and their allies) is going to be dark mirror of the main character and his friends. So, one of the opponents might be a chef who treats his assistants badly (highlighting how well our hero treats his assistant chefs), another one might use frozen food and premade food in his cooking (emphasizing the importance of fresh ingredients and making your own components), and yet another opponent might belittle their customers (showing how important a chef's connection with the people who eat their food is).

As you can see, each of these opponents is there to represent a character who took the wrong route to get to the same place the main character is trying to get, and as a result teaches the audience about what makes the main character a good example of whatever they are. Of course, there can also be opponents who highlight what the main character is doing wrong as well, and act as positive examples of doing things the right way. Your main character isn't perfect, and having opponents that highlight their flaws can help to show how much they need to grow, or how they learned to grow in the right ways.

Naturally, and this is especially true in longer stories, you should try to mix up your opponents to make them interesting, both visually and in the way they're a mirror of the lead. Try not to let two opponents who are similar to each other face the lead back to back. For example, in the above story about the chef, you wouldn't put the opponent who treats his crew badly up right after the one who disdains his customers because they're both about the chef's attitude. You'd need to mix a few chefs with other flaws in between, or present them under very different circumstances so the audience doesn't notice their similarities so easily. (One might be a food truck chef on the mean streets, and the other a rich girl working on a cruise ship, for example.)

Main Opponents

In serials and longer stories like novels or novel series, there is often a special kind of Active Opponent- the Main Opponent. Main Opponents are extremely important to the story, and without handling them properly the whole thing can fall apart. They have several jobs in the story, but the most important is to act as the final opponent the lead must overcome to finish the story. When the lead defeats the Main Opponent, the story is effectively over. They act as a physical representation of the final goal the main character must overcome to win, and by defeating them the audience knows when the story has reached its grand finale.

However, the Main Opponents normally also represents something else- they represent the final major flaw in the Main Character that they must overcome to achieve their goal and fulfill their need. Just as the regular opponents represent wrong ways to approach the theme of the story, the Main Opponent represents the most major way that someone can get the theme wrong. They represent a different way of thinking about the world, and an approach that is the exact opposite to that of the main character.

What does that mean?

Well, most commonly in genre fiction, it usually means that the Main Opponent views the activity they and the lead do as a means to achieve power or control over others. This contrasts with the lead's approach that the activity is there to unite people and bring peace through competition and mutual understanding, as opposed to putting one person in charge.

So, in our great chef example above, the lead chef will want to spread the joy of cooking to everyone, while the Main Opponent chef will consider cooking a tool to get close to the rich and powerful and build a restaurant empire. But, in the end, the lead chef will win because of the things he gained by cooking from his heart, as opposed to the Main Opponent chef whose assistants will abandon him at a crucial moment because of how badly he's treated them in single minded pursuit of his goals.

In serials, the Main Opponent is also usually a growing, developing character as the story goes on. Most often they start the story stuck a few steps ahead of the lead in some way, but their encounters with the lead help them break free of their own limitations and start to rapidly advance again. You don't always have to do it this way, but this way tends to produce very popular Main Opponents who are seen by the audience as misguided heroes in their own right. Then, when the lead and Main Opponent finally do come into direct conflict, the tension is ramped even higher, because the audience knows just what both sides can do, and are waiting to see what happens and who comes out on top.

This is also why you will sometimes see main opponents who are rivals as opposed to villains. A rival is a version of the hero who is admirable, but making a mistake or taking the wrong path for their own reasons, and can even be friends with the lead. A villain is an opponent who knows they're doing the wrong thing but either don't care, or are doing it on purpose out of malice or anger. Audiences love to root for rivals, and it's easier to do stories where the lead and their rival team up against a third party (always a crowd pleaser), while the lead and a villain will be oil and water who want nothing to do with each other.

SUPPORT CHARACTERS

The need for a supporting cast should never be underestimated. Many stories are defined by their supporting cast, who basically represent the main character's connections to the world and society they live in. They are the anchor to the world around the character, and they reflect both the main character and the themes of the story in some way.

Most commonly support characters serve six different roles.

1. **Ally**- This is usually the "best friend" character who is there to cheer the character on and keep them in the story. They get the main character to talk so that the audience can hear the character's thoughts, and they often help to direct the character to think in ways connected to the story by asking questions.
2. **Motivator**- This is a character who helps to keep the story going by motivating the character to act and pursue their goal. Sometimes this character IS the goal, in the case of the Love Interest (see below), and

sometimes they're a boss who tells the character what to do, or a child who gets kidnapped by a monster the character must rescue. Whoever they are, they help to make the story move and keep the main character from sitting on their butt.

3. **Resource**- This is the character that provides the main character (and audience) with the information they need to understand what's happening and keep the main character in play. It can also be the character that provides the main character with the things they need in the story to do what they need to do. This can be the teacher or mentor, the brainy best friend, the starship's science officer, the gunsmith, the gadgeteer, or the mysterious supplier of magical spells. Someone who is there to supply the character with what they need, and need to know, to complete their goals.

4. **Innocent**- This is a character that the main character needs to teach something to, or help to develop in some way. Most often this type of character pops up in stories where the main character is an unchanging larger than life figure who changes the world by showing the right way to live and exemplifying the theme of the story. In those stories, the Innocent is the one learning the truth of the story's theme from the main character, who already knows and lives that truth every day. Sometimes this character acts as a Motivator, but they're more than that, they're often the audience's surrogate when the main character is too unique to be relatable (in which case, they're often the main character, and the larger than life hero is the protagonist).

5. **Catalyst**- This character serves to change the main character's life by becoming part of it, often creating Story Motivations (see above). This can be the new kid in class, a new love, a murder victim, a person in need of help, or anyone else who transforms the main character's life just by walking in the door. They're the cause of the character's world turning upside down, and usually enter the story right at the beginning to kick the whole thing off. Sometimes they're the Motivator of the story, but sometimes they're just the spark that sets off an inferno, either way, they're bringers of change.

6. **Comic Relief**- If a story is dark or tense, sometimes there needs to be a little sunshine and lighter moments to help balance things out. In that case, someone has to be there to make the jokes that lets the tension drop a bit or make the characters (and audience) chuckle. Serious main characters need a foil who isn't so serious to balance them out and keep the tone lighter, and sometimes the funny character delivers the lessons and hard truths of the story in the most entertaining ways.

Often supporting characters play more than one of these roles, and one person can even be all six of the roles in a story. These roles can also shift around between stories as characters change and develop between multiple stories or books, but whatever roles the characters play they should stick with those roles within a single story once you introduce them to the audience as playing that role. If they do change roles, there should be a good reason for it within the story and it shouldn't happen out of the blue. (The best friend shouldn't suddenly turn out to be rich at the end of the story when the character needs money unless it was hinted at or established earlier in the story.)

There are also two jobs of supporting characters which deserve special attention: Foils and Love Interests.

Foils

Some character roles are in stories just to teach us about the main character, and those characters are called Foils. The simplest way to think of a foil is as a mirror image of some aspect of the main character which shows us the main character's qualities by presenting the audience with the opposite. So, the character who is slow shows us how fast the lead is, while the character who is cowardly shows us how brave the lead is, and the character who is handsome lets us know how unattractive the lead is by how people treat them differently.

Most of the main character's supporting cast should be a foil to that character in some way because it makes them more interesting and gives them another job in the story. It also makes them easier to define as characters because you can think about what the main character has and what they don't have, and then create characters which have or don't have those attributes. (Rich/Poor, Skilled/Unskilled, Confident/Cautious, etc.) Or, in a more complex story, the foils might (also) represent different ways of looking at the same issue the main character faces. Diverse ways of dealing with a demanding situation, for example, such as the different approaches students might take when preparing for a difficult test- daily study, study at the last minute, group study, studying alone, drawing infographics, cheating, etc.

Finally, Foils can also represent alternate ways of approaching the central theme or moral argument of the story. If the story is about the right way to be a police officer, then the other characters will represent the other right ways besides the one the main character takes, and maybe the wrong ways as well. (Foil characters aren't always allies, they can also be opponents too.)

Speaking of opponents, major opponents (and the Main Opponent) will often have a supporting cast around them as well who are also functioning as Foils. The major opponent's supporting cast aren't just there to help the opponent work against the lead, but also teach us about the major opponent through their interactions. Often a major opponent's supporters are reflections of them, and the audience knows this unconsciously. If the people around a major opponent are dangerous and scary, it makes their boss twice as intimidating. On the other hand, if the major opponent is surrounded by fools, no matter how skilled or smart the major opponent may be, the audience will think they are an idiot because that's who they've chosen as their supporters.

Love Interests

Technically, Love Interests are just another type of Motivator character, but they're so significant that they're worthy of special attention. The Love Interest is a character who has four basic functions in stories- motivator, humanizer, end goal, and marketing device.

First, they function to motivate the main character by giving them a prize at the end of the story to work towards. As Psychologist Abraham Maslow said, almost everyone wants to be loved (or at least have sex), and that's one of the most primal rewards a character in a story can get. By offering the Love Interest as a reward, it gives the lead extra motivation (or sometimes their main motivation) for doing what they do, and it's a believable one that humanizes them and connects them to the audience because the audience has probably done stupid things for love (or sex) too.

Not only that, it makes a great symbolic end goal that shows that the main character has gone through their problems and is ready to enter a new world and a new life. Once the main character and the love interest kiss (or hold hands, or drive away together...) we know that the story is effectively over and the world is returning to normal, or at least the new normal for the character(s). They have found happiness, and are ready to move on (Roll credits!)

And that end scene also serves another purpose- marketing. The storyteller often wants the audience to leave feeling happy and satisfied so they'll come back again, or at least tell their friends they enjoyed the story on social media. By having a love interest character who connects with the main character at the end, the story reinforces the idea that the perfect person is out there for everyone, and by doing that it makes the audience feel happy and positive about their own life. Finally, Love Interests also add a great excuse to include an attractive person in the cast which can mean a real boost in sales or interest in visual mediums like film and comics.

So, while not every story needs (or should have) a Love Interest character, they do play a significant role in most stories, and that role should be considered by writers when planning stories. Often, it's best to combine them with other roles in the story, however, because as with most characters they won't add much if they only exist to do one thing in the story. (Also, it gives the hot person more screen time, to the joy of their fans and your sales.)

In Summary

All six support character roles can naturally be filled by different characters as the story goes on (there may even be more than one Love Interest), and these roles can even move around between stories. In the first story a character may be an opponent, then a rival in the second, then an ally in the third, and finally even a love interest in the last adventure! The important thing to keep in mind is that every character in a story should be there for clear purpose that supports the story being told.

Lastly, when it comes to the number of characters in a story, it's generally not a good idea to let your casts expand beyond 4-6 major characters (leads, opponents, support) in any story. Any more than that will make the audience work to keep track of everyone and it becomes harder to give all the characters something to do and make them significant in the story. However, that rule of thumb only applies per lead, and by the single story being told. So, if there are two separated lead characters, they might each have their own supporting cast of 4-5 major characters, and this might only apply for a single story in a series as opposed to the series as whole.

That doesn't mean you can't have more people in your setting or world, however, just that there should be a limited number of major or significant characters. The rest of the world should be populated with the final type of character to be discussed...

BACKGROUND CHARACTERS

These are the characters that fill out the rest of the story but who don't play any of the above roles except maybe for a scene or two at most. These are the redshirts, the merchants, the tavern servers, the fellow pilots and the collateral damage victims. The people who might have a few colorful lines, or are there to give a limited viewpoint or perspective on a scene or event that can't be given another way. The Extras, the NPCs, the faceless masses, the... well, you get the point.

Generally, there's not much to say about these folks, except that the writer should remember that they function as representatives of the setting. They are the living embodiments of the world the character lives in, and so every one of them tells the audience lots of information about the world and the major characters' places in it. They will often set the tone of the story, act as minor foils to let us know more about the main characters, and add color to the world they inhabit.

From a writer's perspective, it's generally best to limit these characters to archetypes and not to spend too much time on them. If they're a police officer, then have them act like a typical police officer in that situation, and then move on in the story and events. That is, unless they're a corrupt police officer and there to show that the police in that setting are corrupt, in which case they should act like a corrupt police officer to show the audience the current nature of the organization they represent. Only give them the detail they need to fill their roles, and then let them do their jobs. That's what they're there for, after all.

CHARACTER DETAILS

Speaking of details, some writers struggle with how much detail to give the characters in their stories. They're not sure how much or little description they should give, or what details should be included and which ones should be left out. On this topic, the answers are of course- as much as you need to, and as much as you want to.

That said, there are a few best practices in this area as well.

First, the more detail you give a character, the more distinct they will become in the minds of the audience. On a subconscious level, this means two things- 1) the audience will assume that the character is important to the story in relation to how much detail you give them, and 2) the more detail you give them, the more separate from the audience they will become. The first point means that you should limit your details to the important characters and not detail every single person your characters meet because you'll confuse your audience. The second point means that the more detailed you make the character, the harder it will be for the audience to bond with them.

Comics and animation are good examples of this- go and look at the lead characters and you'll discover their designs are usually very simple in relation to the rest of the cast. Distinctive in a few key ways, but overall very simple in design. Meanwhile, the Main Opponents they face are usually very finely detailed, which is to show the audience that they are not relatable and keep the audience from closely connecting with them. The opponents will have hard, distinctive features that make them unique, while the main characters have softer designs with less lines and more common styles of clothing and hair. (See Scott McCloud's *Understanding Comics* for more on this fascinating topic.)

In written fiction, this often results in main characters who have only the simplest or briefest of descriptions (some books never tell us what their leads look like at all!) and limited traits so that the reader can fill in the rest of the details on their own and feel more connected with the lead characters. Then, the supporting cast will be more detailed depending on how close they are to the lead character, and the opponents will be very distinctive and detailed.

So, when deciding how to present your characters, keep in mind that if you want the character to be closer to the reader then focus on the little things that make them special, while if you want the character to be more distant then focus on the big details that make them special. It's a range, not an either-or, and deciding where on the sliding scale you put your characters can have a great psychological effect on your audience, so use it wisely.

THE PEOPLE VS. MARY SUE

Finally, there is one issue that keeps coming up for many new writers, and that's how much of yourself to put into the lead characters. Many of you have likely heard of the Internet meme about "Mary Sue" (or occasionally "Marty Stu"), the shiningly perfect beloved writer avatar who can do no wrong and is literally the writer putting themselves into the story and glorying in their fantasies. This is pretty common in fan fiction (where the writer introduces themselves under another name as a new student at Hogwarts, or as a new Jedi, Vampire, Avenger, or whatever, and then is better than everyone else in the story and can do no wrong as they eclipse the rest of the story's original cast). And Mary Sues aren't uncommon in regular genre fiction as well, where some stories read like a writer's dreams come to life as they kick butt and find romance.

And, to tell the truth, there's nothing wrong with that, because the reality is that all lead characters are reflections of the writer who created them (or is currently writing them). The same is true for the supporting cast, and even the world they live in- all of which are a reflection of the wants, needs, views and ideas bouncing around inside the head of the writer. Everything in a story is part of the person who writes it, and writers shouldn't be trying to desperately erase any trace of themselves from their stories because that's like trying to erase your own body.

Lastly, a big part of writing fiction is about the writer living out their dreams and seeing their ideas come to life, and this generates a lot of their passion and enthusiasm for writing and keeps them working on projects when the going gets hard. For some other writers, playing out personal "what if" situations from their lives is a big part of why they write, so telling them to not put themselves into the story would be pointless.

All that said, there's a reason audiences dislike Mary Sue type characters.

We experience fiction to learn about how others deal with adversity and overcome obstacles to achieve goals, and a lot of what makes stories interesting is the challenge the characters face. It's what makes the story dramatic and interesting- and is exactly what most stories about Mary Sues lack. When a writer is writing a Mary Sue, the character isn't being challenged (because they're good at everything), and they're not really solving problems (because they're just going to win anyways). They also don't usually grow or develop (because then they'd stop being the writer), and so they're the worst kind of unchanging character who just wanders through the world without doing much except being awesome.

Now, sometimes in the hands of a skilled writer (or one with a strong imagination), Mary Sue character stories can be pretty entertaining. The character of Conan the Barbarian, for example, was basically a Mary Sue version of his creator Robert E. Howard, but his adventures are so vividly told and glorious that Conan's lack of depth can be forgiven. Similarly, some have said the character of Bella Swan in the *Twilight* books is also a Mary Sue, but her stories touched the hearts of a whole generation of women with their epic vampire love story and the world the author built around those characters. However, for every Conan or Bella, there are thousands or tens of thousands of really crappy wish-fulfillment stories that make people click the "close" button in frustration or dismay.

So, when you can, try to think of your lead characters as being like your children instead of extensions of yourself. Let them be their own person, and grow, and change, and learn, and make lots of mistakes. Let them fail, and then rise up again, and give them difficult lives you wouldn't wish on your worst enemy. Let others hate them as much as admire them, and don't fall into the trap of thinking that your audience will think they are you, or that they will reflect on you. Don't give them your name(s) or initials, and don't make them have all the same likes and dislikes as you have. They are part of you, but they aren't you, and shouldn't be you unless you're writing your autobiography.

On the other hand, love spending time with them, encourage them to try new things, enjoy what they enjoy vicariously, and let them do the things you wish you could. Give them chances to be better than you, and watch as they explore the places you couldn't go, or don't have the courage to. Feel what they feel, and laugh and cry with them, and don't be afraid to let them help you get through the hard times in your life. They will be your friends, they will be your family, and at times they might be your emotional safety valve letting off pressure.

But most of all, they will be a unique expression of you that you can share with the world.

PLOT

For such a short word, the word plot causes a great deal of confusion. It's a short four-letter word, but like many four-letter words it can mean a great many things (both positive and negative) depending on the situation where it's used.

In the chapter on The Building Blocks of Story we already defined what plot actually is- an organized pattern of events which come together to form a story. It's the way in which a character accomplishes their goals as mapped out by the choices they make and the events which happen as they try to reach whatever their objectives are. But that's only the basic definition of plot because plot isn't just a single idea, its many ideas all wrapped up together in the goal of creating greater and more complex stories.

Plot is the result of storytelling evolution- the way we humans have worked towards telling better and more effective stories. It is patterns, structures, and strategies which have developed in the hands of millions of storytellers over the ages, and which are still growing and changing even as you read this. It's a creation of the deep desire in all storytellers to push the form of story as far as it can go and find the Shakespeare Code that will let them write the perfect story.

To keep things simple, however, this book is going to break plot down into two different but interconnected was of looking at plot and its relationship with stories- plot as content, and plot as structure. Both of these are perfectly good ways to look at plot, and depending on your writing style and needs as a writer, you may only like to really focus one or the other, but it's still important to understand both.

So, let's dig into plot!

PLOT AS CONTENT

In his book *Poetics*, the writer Aristotle claimed that there were only three plots in the world, and that all stories are derivations of these three plots:

- Man vs. Man

- Man vs. Himself
- Man vs. Nature

While later writers would add a few more to this list (Man vs. Society, and Man vs. Technology, among others), this is a good example of what we mean when we talk about Plot as Content- plot which tells us what happens in a story. There are many different approaches people have taken when trying to figure out how to tell the best story they can tell.

ONE PLOT TO RULE THEM ALL

To begin with, there are many writers and writing scholars who have followed in Aristotle's footsteps and tried to list all the possible key plots that a writer might use in their stories. For example, late 19th century Italian author Georges Polti claimed that there were only 36 Dramatic Situations and that the vast majority of stories were one of these.

1. Supplication
2. Deliverance
3. Vengeance of a crime
4. Vengeance taken for kindred upon kindred
5. Pursuit
6. Disaster
7. Falling prey to cruelty or misfortune
8. Revolt
9. Daring enterprise
10. Abduction
11. Enigma
12. Obtaining
13. Enmity of kinsmen
14. Rivalry of kinsmen
15. Murderous adultery
16. Madness
17. Fatal imprudence
18. Involuntary crimes of love
19. Slaying of a kinsman unrecognized
20. Self-sacrificing for an ideal

21. Self-sacrifice for kindred
22. All sacrificed for a passion
23. Necessity of sacrificing loved ones
24. Rivalry of superior and inferior
25. Adultery
26. Crimes of love
27. Discovery of the dishonor of a loved one
28. Obstacles to love
29. An enemy loved
30. Ambition
31. Conflict with a god
32. Mistaken jealousy
33. Erroneous judgment
34. Remorse
35. Recovery of a lost one
36. Loss of loved ones

A quick search online will find more detail about each of those if you want to know more, but the point here is that there is a long tradition of writing scholars trying to catalogue the possible number of plots you find in fiction. Even today, you can find books like Blake Snyder's *Save the Cat!* (which includes his 10 Story Genres), The *Seven Basic Plots* (by Christopher Booker), and Ronald B. Tobias' *20 Master Plots: And How to Build Them.* Any of which can give you a strong foundation in the content of the most common plots that we use when telling stories.

However, in truth, there is only one plot which the majority of successful fiction uses, and it was perhaps best outlined in the 1952 *Writers Digest* article, A Fiction Formula That Helped Me Sell 1,000 Stories, by author Lee Floren. In the article, he stated that every story he wrote was based on the following plot, which (whether he knew it or not), is the plot at the heart of most popular fiction.

"An appealing character strives against great odds to attain a worthwhile goal."

A character who the audience can like (or at least appreciate) works hard to accomplish something that the audience too considers an aim worth achieving. This can be something internal like happiness or peace of mind, or something external like building a railroad or saving a city- it doesn't matter as long as the audience would agree that what the main character is trying to do is something they can understand and empathize with.

If this sounds familiar, it should, as this is what most of the stories you read, watch, listen to, or otherwise enjoy are about. It is the single idea which drives most fiction, and connects to something primal in all of us. Not that this is surprising if you think about it, as we consume stories in order to learn about our world through the experiences of others, and what better story is there to learn from than a character trying to accomplish some difficult goal? Especially a one we can relate to the goals and struggles of our own lives?

If there is one central plot to build your stories around, this is it, and when you're looking for ways to turn an interesting idea into a story, remember that people aren't interested in ideas by themselves, they're interested in people struggling with ideas that help or hurt them in whatever goals they're trying to accomplish. Whether this is a man trying to build a bridge, a woman trying to heal a rift between herself and her mother, or a robot trying to decide the fate of the last human on earth. All of these are stories about difficult decisions, choices, and struggles carried out by a character trying to do something we would consider worthy of support.

PLOT AS FORMULA

Another common way that writers have tried to understand what needs to be put in a story is by creating formulas and checklists to describe the key elements of stories. This is different from a story structure (see below) because unlike the more neutral story structures which authors use to organize their work, story formulas and checklists don't always tell you where things need to go, but instead focus on what you need to include to make a story work.

Below is a collection of different approaches writers have taken to creating formulas that allowed them to writer better stories.

THE HERO'S JOURNEY

The grandmaster of story formulas is Joseph Campbell- ironically enough, a man who never intended to write a story formula. A Comparative Mythologist, Campbell was fascinated by myths, legends, and fairy tales, and so devoted his life to their study and analysis. He wrote his findings in a book called *The Hero With a Thousand Faces*, which was based on his belief that all myths and legends have a common set of characters and events which occur within them (which he called the Monomyth). In his book, he outlined those characters and events so that readers could better understand the primal nature of myths and legends.

Naturally, as soon as other writers read it, many of them believed that Campbell had stumbled across the Shakespeare Code, and that his Monomyth was in fact the golden formula for successful storytelling. Writers such as George Lucas saw it as a way to tell a great story, and Lucas consulted with Campbell when he was making his new and upcoming film *Star Wars*. Other writers, like David Adams Leeming, wrote books talking about how Campbell's analysis could be turned into a story structure for popular fiction. And, a young writer working at Disney in the 1990s named Christopher Vogler wrote a seven-page memo describing the Hero's Journey as a template for making the perfect film that became one of the most-read things in Hollywood for years to come.

Vogler's version, which would later be turned into his bestselling book *The Writer's Journey: Mythic Structure for Writers*, has become the handbook for those who believe in the Monomyth's power to bring fiction to life. In it, he turns Campbell's 17 stages that every heroic story should pass through into just 12 stages, and explains them in more straightforward language than Campbell used. Vogler's 12 stages are:

1. Ordinary world – the main character is living a normal life
2. Call to adventure – something happens that makes them leave that normal life
3. Refusal of the call – they don't want to go
4. Meeting with the mentor – a mentor appears who will be their guide into the new world
5. Crossing the first threshold – they do something that starts their journey into the new world
6. Tests, allies and enemies – they face small challenges as they try to accomplish their goals
7. Approach to the inmost cave – they feel confident because they beat the lesser challenges
8. The ordeal – they face a larger challenge which shows them it isn't so easy
9. Reward – they're shown the reward to be theirs if they finish their quest
10. The road back – they prepare for their greatest challenge
11. The resurrection – they face a final great challenge which they must overcome to transform into the new person they're destined to be
12. Return with the elixir – they get home and everyone loves them

Vogler, and Campbell, saw these as the signposts or waypoints which main characters must pass through during a story to experience a full cycle of change and rebirth as a new person. They believe that these stages are universal and that most great stories that resonate with audiences go through some version of them. Some writers have also boiled them down to as few as five stages, and there are countless books and articles on the subject that cover will cover the topic in more detail if you wish to explore The Hero's Journey.

That said, one word of caution about The Hero's Journey, however- not a few of its supporters will claim this this is indeed the Shakespeare Code that tells how to write the perfect story. It's a trap that many writers fall into, since they want to believe that there is a simple secret to writing perfect stories. However, there are two flaws with that claim. One, as we've already covered, the elements of story are far simpler than the stages of a Hero's Journey formula, which means that the Hero's Journey itself is just a way to expand on those basic story elements of subject-action-result. It is just one way, not the only way. And two, if the Hero's Journey was indeed the perfect formula, then Hollywood would have been churning out near-perfect films since the 1990s- something that has definitely not happened.

That said, if you're telling a story about a young person becoming an adult, or someone going on a life-changing odyssey, then The Hero's Journey (at least Vogler's interpretation) is definitely worth looking into. It is a way to give your story a structure that has been proven to work, and which seems to resonate with audiences. It will help guide you with both structure and character, and give you a clear direction which you can use to keep your story on track and moving through a proven set of waypoints as it works its way to the end.

THE LESTER DENT FORMULA

Similarly, you can find many story formulas in books and online which are geared towards specific types of stories. Many of these resemble checklists, or vague outlines, which tell an aspiring writer what they need to include to really make the story sing. One of the best known and most useful of these is the famous Lester Dent Master Pulp Fiction Writing Formula, outlined and used by one of the 20th century's most prolific writers. He used to churn out 159 novels using a variation of this formula (which is actually set up for short stories), and many other people like author Michael Moorcock have used this formula in different ways since it was written long ago.

Here is the formula in its entirety:

"This is one opinion. It is opinion of one who believes in formula and mechanical construction, for a pulp yarn. It is opinion of one believing:

1— Majority of pulps are formula.

2— Most editors who say they don't want formula don't know what they are talking about.

3— Some eds won't buy anything but formula.

Framed over this typewriter, on a bulkhead of my schooner now anchored off a bay in the Caribbean while we attempt to raise a Spanish treasure, is an object which tends to make the convictions mentioned appear to be facts—or an unexpected hallucination.

The object on the bulkhead is a formula, a master plot, for any 6000-word pulp story. It has worked on adventure, detective, western and war-air. It tells exactly where to put everything. It shows definitely just what must happen in each successive thousand words.

No yarn written to the formula has yet failed to sell.

A year or so ago, a rough form of this master plot was handed to a man who still had a first sale to make. If recollection is correct, he sold his next six yarns written to the master plot.

The business of building stories seems not much different from the business of building anything else. The idea is apparently to get materials, get a plan, and go to it.

The rough form of this story plan, this master plot, will follow. But first, it might be a good idea to consider some of the materials.

It seems likely that "character" rates as one of the principal story-making materials. Many a yarn comes back with "Inadequate Characterization" penciled on a rejection slip, and a scribbler works up a headache trying to figure out what the hell that meant. It might help to glance over some barn door variety characterization gags that most professionals use.

A fair idea is to make out a list of characters before starting a yarn. Then it's conceivably a better idea to try to get along with half the list.

For a detective yarn, several characters may be handy, to wit: **One** hero. **One** villain. Various persons to murder. It may not be a sure-fire thing to murder women, some editors being finicky that way. Somebody for the hero to rescue is often handy, too. Female. Not female, though, if the editor has what he is wont to quaintly call a "no woman interest" mag.

Characterizing a story actor consists of giving him some things which make him stick in the reader's mind. Tag him. A tag may be described as something to recognize somebody by. Haile Selassie's sheet and drawers might be called an appearance tag. So might Old John Silver's wooden leg in Treasure Island. And movie comic Joe Brown's big mouth. The idea is to show the tag to the reader so that he may thereby recognize the actor in the story. Instead of marching the character in only by name, parade the tag.

Mannerism tags may cover absent-minded gestures. Perhaps the villain (villainy at this point unknown) is often noted rubbing his eyes when in private or when thinking himself unobserved. At end of yarn, it turns out the color of his eyes has been disguised by the new style glass opticians' cap which fits directly on the eyeball, and cap was irritating his eyes.

It's nice to have tags take a definite bearing on the story. Not all can, however.

Disposition tags should not be overlooked. Is the character a hard guy? Does he love his women and leave 'em—and later help them over the rough spots? This tagging might go on and on and become more and more subtle.

Characters usually have names. Occasionally an author is a literary Argus who writes a yarn carrying the actors through by their tags alone, then goes back and names them. This procedure is not necessarily to be advised, except a time or two for practice.

It is not a bad idea to use some system in picking names. Two characters in the yarn may not necessarily need names which look alike. Confusing the reader can be left to villains. If the hero's name is Johnson, "J" and "son" names for the others might be avoided. Too, it may not be the best idea to go in for all very short names exclusively. And a worse idea is to go in for all long ones. Telephone books are full of names, but it's an idea to twist them around, selecting a first name here, second one there. If nothing better is at hand, a newspaper, possibly the obit page, can help.

Now, about that master plot. It's a formula, a blueprint for any 6000-word yarn.

A rough outline can be laid out with the typewriter, although some mental wizards may do it all in their heads. About a page of outline to every ten pages of finished yarn might serve.

This is a formula, a master plot, for any 6000 word pulp story. It has worked on adventure, detective, western and war-air. It tells exactly where to put everything. It shows definitely just what must happen in each successive thousand words.

The business of building stories seems not much different from the business of building anything else.

Here's how it starts:

1. A DIFFERENT MURDER METHOD FOR VILLAIN TO USE
2. A DIFFERENT THING FOR VILLAIN TO BE SEEKING
3. A DIFFERENT LOCALE
4. A MENACE WHICH IS TO HANG LIKE A CLOUD OVER HERO

One of these DIFFERENT things would be nice, two better, three swell. It may help if they are fully in mind before tackling the rest.

A different murder method could be–different. Thinking of shooting, knifing, hydrocyanic, garroting, poison needles, scorpions, a few others, and writing them on paper gets them where they may suggest something. Scorpions and their poison bite?

Maybe mosquitos or flies treated with deadly germs?

If the victims are killed by ordinary methods, but found under strange and identical circumstances each time, it might serve, the reader of course not knowing until the end, that the method of murder is ordinary. Scribes who have their villain's victims found with butterflies, spiders or bats stamped on them could conceivably be flirting with this gag.

Probably it won't do a lot of good to be too odd, fanciful or grotesque with murder methods.

The different thing for the villain to be after might be something other than jewels, the stolen bank loot, the pearls, or some other old ones.

Here, again one might get too bizarre.

Unique locale? Easy. Selecting one that fits in with the murder method and the treasure–thing that villain wants–makes it simpler, and it's also nice to use a familiar one, a place where you've lived or worked. So many pulpateers don't. It sometimes saves embarrassment to know nearly as much about the locale as the editor, or enough to fool him.

Here's a nifty much used in faking local color. For a story laid in Egypt, say, author finds a book titled "Conversational Egyptian Easily Learned," or something like that. He wants a character to ask in Egyptian, "What's the matter?" He looks in the book and finds, "El khabar, eyh?" To keep the reader from getting dizzy, it's perhaps wise to make it clear in some fashion, just what that means. Occasionally the text will tell this, or someone can repeat it in English. But it's a doubtful move to stop and tell the reader in so many words the English translation.

The writer learns they have palm trees in Egypt. He looks in the book, finds the Egyptian for palm trees, and uses that. This kids editors and readers into thinking he knows something about Egypt.

Here's the second installment of the master plot.

Divide the 6000 word yarn into four 1500 word parts. In each 1500 word part, put the following:

FIRST 1500 WORDS

1. First line, or as near thereto as possible, introduce the hero and swat him with a fistful of trouble. Hint at a mystery, a menace or a problem to be solved–something the hero has to cope with.
2. The hero pitches in to cope with his fistful of trouble. (He tries to fathom the mystery, defeat the menace, or solve the problem.)

3. Introduce ALL the other characters as soon as possible. Bring them on in action.
4. Hero's endevours land him in an actual physical conflict near the end of the first 1500 words.
5. Near the end of first 1500 words, there is a complete surprise twist in the plot development.

SO FAR: Does it have SUSPENSE? Is there a MENACE to the hero? Does everything happen logically?

At this point, it might help to recall that action should do something besides advance the hero over the scenery. Suppose the hero has learned the dastards of villains have seized somebody named Eloise, who can explain the secret of what is behind all these sinister events. The hero corners villains, they fight, and villains get away. Not so hot.

Hero should accomplish something with his tearing around, if only to rescue Eloise, and surprise! Eloise is a ring-tailed monkey. The hero counts the rings on Eloise's tail, if nothing better comes to mind. They're not real. The rings are painted there. Why?

SECOND 1500 WORDS

1. Shovel more grief onto the hero.
2. Hero, being heroic, struggles, and his struggles lead up to:
3. Another physical conflict.
4. A surprising plot twist to end the 1500 words.

NOW: Does second part have SUSPENSE? Does the MENACE grow like a black cloud? Is the hero getting it in the neck? Is the second part logical?

DON'T TELL ABOUT IT! Show how the thing looked. This is one of the secrets of writing; never tell the reader–show him. (He trembles, roving eyes, slackened jaw, and such.) MAKE THE READER SEE HIM.

When writing, it helps to get at least one minor surprise to the printed page. It is reasonable to to expect these minor surprises to sort of inveigle the reader into keeping on. They need not be such profound efforts. One method of accomplishing one now and then is to be gently misleading. Hero is examining the murder room. The door behind him begins slowly to open. He does not see it. He conducts his examination blissfully. Door eases open, wider and wider, until–surprise! The glass pane falls out of the big window across the room. It must have fallen slowly, and air blowing into the room caused the door to open. Then what the heck made the pane fall so slowly? More mystery.

Characterizing a story actor consists of giving him some things which make him stick in the reader's mind. TAG HIM.

BUILD YOUR PLOTS SO THAT ACTION CAN BE CONTINUOUS.

THIRD 1500 WORDS

1. Shovel the grief onto the hero.
2. Hero makes some headway, and corners the villain or somebody in:
3. A physical conflict.
4. A surprising plot twist, in which the hero preferably gets it in the neck bad, to end the 1500 words.

DOES: It still have SUSPENSE? The MENACE getting blacker? The hero finds himself in a hell of a fix? It all happen logically?

These outlines or master formulas are only something to make you certain of inserting some physical conflict, and some genuine plot twists, with a little suspense and menace thrown in. Without them, there is no pulp story.

These physical conflicts in each part might be DIFFERENT, too. If one fight is with fists, that can take care of the pugilism until next the next yarn. Same for poison gas and swords. There may, naturally, be exceptions. A hero with a peculiar punch, or a quick draw, might use it more than once.

The idea is to avoid monotony.

ACTION: Vivid, swift, no words wasted. Create suspense, make the reader see and feel the action.

ATMOSPHERE: Hear, smell, see, feel and taste.

DESCRIPTION: Trees, wind, scenery and water.

THE SECRET OF ALL WRITING IS TO MAKE EVERY WORD COUNT.

FOURTH 1500 WORDS

1. Shovel the difficulties more thickly upon the hero.
2. Get the hero almost buried in his troubles. (Figuratively, the villain has him prisoner and has him framed for a murder rap; the girl is presumably dead, everything is lost, and the DIFFERENT murder method is about to dispose of the suffering protagonist.)
3. The hero extricates himself using HIS OWN SKILL, training or brawn.
4. The mysteries remaining–one big one held over to this point will help grip interest–are cleared up in course of final conflict as hero takes the situation in hand.
5. Final twist, a big surprise, (This can be the villain turning out to be the unexpected person, having the "Treasure" be a dud, etc.)
6. The snapper, the punch line to end it.

HAS: The SUSPENSE held out to the last line? The MENACE held out to the last? Everything been explained? It all happen logically? Is the Punch Line enough to leave the reader with that WARM FEELING? Did God kill the villain? Or the hero?"

And there you have it, one of the greatest four-act fiction outlines ever written. Play with it, try it out for a test run, and don't be afraid to change those word counts. Using 1500 words an act is great for a short story, but a novel could easily be 15,000 words an act, and hit all of the same story beats. It's all about dividing your story into four manageable quarters and then packing them full of interesting events.

FRANK GRUBER'S CHECKLIST

Not all outlines are so specific about what goes where- some are more like checklists. A good example of this is pulp writer Frank Gruber's "Fool-proof 11 Point Formula for Mystery Short Stories" which he included in his memoirs of the writing trade- *The Pulp Jungle*.

Here is the whole list with his introduction:

"I used to analyze stories. What elements were required? After a period of time I evolved a formula for mystery short stories. It consisted of eleven elements. With those eleven elements in a mystery plot, I could not miss. I used to work out each element at a time, concentrating on one until I had it licked, the going on to the next. Most writers of mysteries inject the eleven elements into their stories anyway, but by putting them down one at a time I became conscious of them. Once I had worked out these eleven elements, the job of coming up with plots for mystery stories was greatly simplified.

I did not create this 11-point formula at one time. I evolved it over a period of about two years beginning back in 1934. I had perfected it by about the middle of 1936.

To this day I claim that this plot formula is foolproof. You can write a perfectly salable mystery story with perhaps only seven or eight of these elements, but get them all into a story and you cannot miss. Here are the eleven elements:

1. THE HERO. A hero must be colorful. He must have an occupation that is colorful or he must be a colorful person. In general, I have followed the theory that a regular policeman or detective is not colorful. Just think a moment

about the greatest detective in all detective fiction - Sherlock Holmes - and you will quickly grasp what I mean by colorful.

2. THEME. This, to me, is the most important element of any mystery story plot. By theme I mean subject matter, what the story is about in addition to, over and above, the ACTUAL MURDER plot. To illustrate:

   "Death and the Main" is about fighting cocks. I give a reasonably inside account of how gamecocks are raised, how they are fought, etc. This is knowledge not possessed by the average reader and believe me, I did not know it until I read up on the subject, for the purpose of this story.

   My book, *The Lock & the Key*, was about locksmiths. A liberal education in making locks and keys was thrown into the murder plot. I knew absolutely nothing about locks and keys until I did research on the subject. I know no more than is in the book.

   If you have ever read Dorothy Sayers' excellent English mysteries, you will find that THEME figures superbly. In *The Nine Tailors*, the reader earns all about church bells, the art of bell-ringing, etc. In *Murder Must Advertise*, Miss Sayres discusses advertising in all its phases.

   HOWEVER . . . knowledge of a subject should be used sparingly. The mystery reader may not be as interested in the subject as you are.

3. VILLAIN. Let's face it, the hero of detective fiction is a Superman. The villain must therefore be a super-Superman or have plenty of assistants. The odds must ALWAYS be against the hero.
4. BACKGROUND. The story must be played against a colorful or unusual background. The streets of a big city are not necessarily colorful. If they're not, make them so.
5. MURDER METHOD. Here again, the "unusual" should be considered. Shooting, stabbing, etc. are acceptable, but the circumstances surrounding them should be "unusual."
6. MOTIVE. Actually, there are only two reasons for murder - hate and greed, but there are many subdivisions of these and the motive should be as unusual as possible.
7. CLUE. Somewhere in the story, there must be a clue for the alert reader. Sure, try to fool the reader, but the clue must be there if the reader should want to check back on you, after the story is over.
8. TRICK. In the grand finale, when all seems lost, when the hero cannot possibly win out, he must snatch victory from apparent defeat. By a trick... and here the word "unusual" applies.
9. ACTION. The story must have pace and movement. It must not consist of talk, talk, talk, about the missing button, etc.
10. CLIMAX. A grand, smashing climax is necessary. Unusual.

11. EMOTION. The hero should be personally involved in some manner. He should be doing this, over and beyond the call of duty. Or, beyond the money paid him for doing it."

As you can see, this gives a perfectly clear list of elements of what Gruber saw as was needed for a well-formed mystery story that would sell. It could also apply to many other styles and types of writing, but the point is that all story formulas are geared towards a specific kind of story, and as a writer you must be aware of this when you use them because it will affect the stories you tell. And, not all writers work well with all formulas, either. You might be trying to use a current, hot "can't miss" formula for your book and find it doesn't work for you, but that's not because you're a bad writer- it's because that particular formula doesn't match up with your storytelling style.

You can find a collection of links to story formulas at robynpaterson.com, if you want to see how other writers have tried to tackle the situation.

PLOT AS STRUCTURE

If Plot as Content answers the question "What happens?" then Plot as Structure answers the question "When does it happen?" Luckily for you, the writer, unlike when we're discussing plot in terms of content, which can play out an unlimited number of ways, Plot as Structure is actually pretty simple. As we covered in the chapter on The Building Blocks of Story, there is really only one story structure- the three-act structure, and almost all other story structures are simply variations or more detailed versions of it. So, as long as you master the three-act structure, you're pretty much set in terms of being able to put together at least a basic story. Organizing more complex stories takes more practice and effort, but just so long as you master the three-act structure, you're good to go.

That said, you can find many different versions of the three-act structure around, and some of them (like the first one below) are so common that many people think they ARE the one true version of the three-act structure. However, all they really are is just three-act stories which have been modified to suit a particular style or purpose like writing books or films. The truth is, as long as a story conforms to the three parts of the basic three-act story unit, it's a "correct" story and is being told correctly. Don't get too hung up on whether your story includes all the extra parts, or where they go, because that's just one writer's way of expanding the structure to suit their needs, not a golden rule that all writers must follow.

However, looking at how different writing approaches use the three-act structure can teach us a lot about it, and the ways it can be used. So, let's look at a few of the more common ones.

AMERICAN (HOLLYWOOD) THREE-ACT STRUCTURE

One of the most common story structures used by Americans (and most of the Western world) in comics, films, television, and other fiction, is this classic version of the three-act structure with some extra parts that American writers have mixed in over the years to give it a flavor all its own. It is especially popular in Hollywood, where thanks to writers like Syd Field, it's become the gold standard for studio storytelling.

Here's what it looks like graphed out...

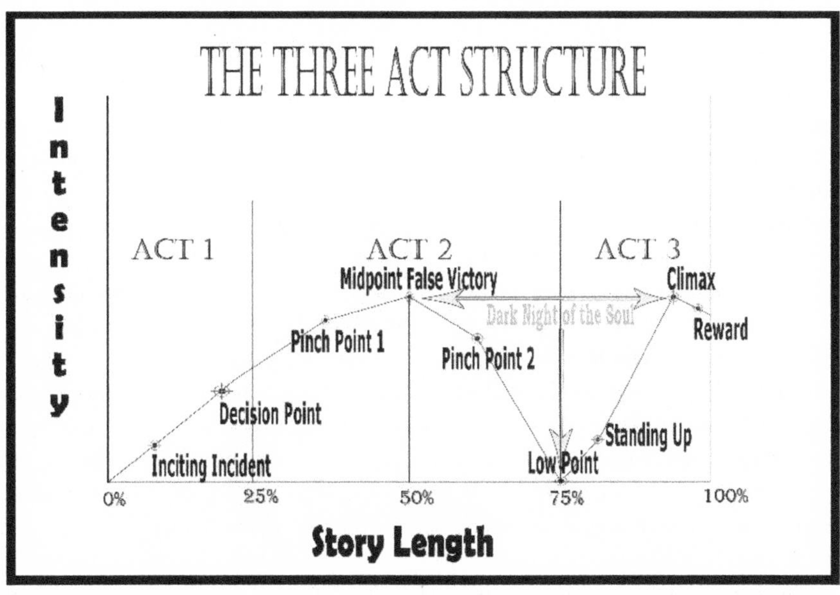

As you can see, it's the basic Three Act Structure, but there are a lot of extra smaller parts to it that film writers have added to act as goalposts and milestones and keep the story on track.

Let's go through it and explain what each of those terms mean.

Act One

The characters are introduced, along with the setting, situations and information the audience needs to know to set the story up. There are also two major events that occur during Act One in most stories:

The Inciting Incident is an event which occurs near the beginning of Act One that sets the story into motion. This is not something that the main character would choose to have happen, but is an outside event that happens and sets off a chain of events which will carry us to the end of the story. This event affects the main character in some way, and uproots the main character from their life to bring them into the plot. (It doesn't have to happen TO the main character, however, as in a crime story it's someone getting murdered, or a body being found, for example.)

The Decision Point (aka Turning/Plot Point One in many screenwriting books) occurs near the end of Act One and this is the point where the character actively chooses to become part of the story based on their available options. Prior to this they were unsure if they wanted to become an active part of the story, or how to handle their situation, but after this they are 100% involved in the story, and will now begin trying to solve the story's central challenge.

Act Two

The characters are now trying to accomplish their goals, and this is where most of the action and events occur as the characters try different ways to reach their goals and overcome obstacles between themselves and those goals. This section includes four different major points in most stories:

Pinch Point 1 is the first major challenge that the main character faces and must figure out how to solve.

The **Midpoint False Victory** is when the main character has overcome the challenge of the first Pinch Point and is feeling like they can do this. They feel they're on the right road, and the end is now in sight.

Pinch Point 2 is the second major obstacle that the main character faces, and one which looks nearly impossible overcome. This is usually when the Main Opponent shows their real power or some aspect of the Main Opponent's real power is revealed so the hero and audience now truly understand how hard it's going to be to win. Allies get injured or die, betrayals happen, and the hero's plans turn into a big flaming wreck.

The **Low Point** (aka Turning or Plot Point Two) is the point where the main character truly faces the possibility of their own failure and reaches their emotionally lowest point in the story. This point of the story is the moment when the character faces the possibility of real failure and defeat.

The Dark Night of the Soul – See Below.

Act Three

As the characters enter Act Three, they are in very poor condition and are doing their best to just keep going. They have faced their lowest, darkest moment, and despite that they are still trying to accomplish their goal. Often, the dark moment has taught them what's really important in life or made them reflect on their motivations. This act is where the Climax will happen, and the character will come face-to-face with the Main Opponent of the story and must find out if they're capable of defeating them. There are typically three major moments that occur during the third act of most stories:

Standing Up is when the character has decided they are not going to stay down and are going to make an effort to accomplish their goal no matter what. Armed with a new sense of purpose, their courage, their conviction, and whatever else they have mustered, they again march toward their goal.

The Climax is when they find themselves face-to-face with the Main Opponent, and meet them with their ideas, their ideals, and sometimes their fists. This represents the moment where the main character must overcome any weakness which was holding them back and give 110% in order to win.

The Reward is the end of the story, where the character is given a reward of some kind for defeating the Main Opponent and becoming the person they could always be if they only overcame their personal flaws. This may be a literal reward, or the affection of the Love Interest, or anything else that will symbolize the character being rewarded for their efforts. Sometimes they start a new life, sometimes they are just returning to the person they were at the beginning, but regardless of which one, the world is a better place for them.

This story structure likely evolved out of a Christian traditional story structure called a Morality Play. In many Morality Plays, the innocent main character is tempted away from the right way of living by sin, discovers its dark side, sinks into despair, finds God, and then recovers their life. The idea being to teach the audience not to fall prey to the wicked temptations sent by the Devil, and to remember that God is always there to show them the way if they will only accept him into their hearts.

In the modern three-act version, the main character of the story has some weakness or flaw that is hurting them and/or the people around them. They refuse to deal with that flaw, however, and so when they reach their Decision Point at the start of the story they pick the wrong way to solve the problem. This method seems to work well enough, and gets them past Pinch Point 1 and to their False Victory at the midpoint. However, since they didn't really deal with their own flaws, the Main Opponent shows up and exploits that weakness to crush them at the second Pinch Point and leave them at their Low Point at the start of Act 2. The main character then accepts what they were doing was the wrong way, picks the right path and Stands Up to try again. This leads them to the Climax, where they are now fighting the right way, and so they win, and get their Reward- proving that this is the right way to live.

Used like this, the three-act structure is a teaching structure which is able to show almost any lesson, and the underlying theme helps to give the story shape and subtext. The story is no longer just about a character trying to accomplish a goal, but a parable and life lesson that can resonate with the audience and reinforce the values of society. If the theme of the story is that slavery hurts the human spirit, then the character will start the story thinking slavery is okay, but then at their Low Point will accept that thinking slavery was reasonable was what brought them to this bad situation and change their thinking. If the writer wants to show the evils of gambling, the character will try to solve their problems at the Decision Point by gambling, seem to have some success, discover they just made things worse, and then accept that gambling is the problem and not the solution, before they then Stand Up and try to fix their life.

The American three-act structure is a tool for dramatizing life lessons, and used that way, it can be quite powerful. But, it has an extra special move that makes it even more effective...

The Dark Night of the Soul

The dip between the Midpoint False Victory and the Climax that is referred to as the Dark Night of the Soul is perhaps one of the American Three Act Structure's most important features. It is here where the character comes face to face with their own weakness and flaws, usually because those very flaws caused the character to stumble and fall prey to their enemies.

As noted above, the Dark Night is there to teach the audience a lesson, but it has some other benefits as well, which is why so many stories use it. First, it enhances the excitement of the story, as by having the main character fall so close to failure, it makes their rise back up even more exciting for the audience and leads to a bigger and more emotional finish. The audience has now gone on a little roller-coaster ride with the main character and bonded with them through their ups and downs, and it makes the climax all the sweeter as they face it together. And, second, the Dark Night also creates a feeling of depth to the main character, since we've gone through both their highs and lows with them, and they feel more real to the audience because of it.

There is, however, a downside to using the Dark Night of the Soul, which is that it's a great moment of transformation for the character. This might not sound like much of a disadvantage until you try to write 12 stories a year for decades about the same Superhero who isn't allowed to change but are still trying to use this story structure, Dark Night and all. Or perhaps you're writing a sequel novel or movie to a big hit, and your single rule is that the main character can't actually change because the character is what made the first movie such a big hit and you don't want to risk killing the golden goose.

Unchanging lead characters and the Dark Night don't mix well together, but there are four possible ways you can do it:

- The Dim Evening of the Soul – The first method for using the Dark Night with characters who can't actually change is to remember that the change doesn't always need to be huge. The character might just discover that some relatively little thing was tripping them up, like their inability to organize their life, and by fixing that small thing they're able to pull out of their tailspin. Or maybe the character was just lacking information, and once they find that information they now have the key to put everything together and solve their problems. While these smaller changes might not be transforming, they can let the character go through the motions of facing a personal crisis while still not actually needing to change anything significant in the end.
- The Reset Button – The character undergoes the full story, Dark Night and all, and then when it's time for the next story the character is back to their old ways again, the transformation from the last story having failed to stick once the story was over. Sometimes this works, but usually audiences hate this because it makes all the effort of the previous story feel like wasted time, and it's like you're cheating them over and over. ("This time they'll transform for real! Honest!") Generally, it only works well in Situation Comedies where neither the audience or the makers of the show really want the characters to change, because the point of the show is a comfortable world which never changes.
- Shifting the Transformation – The third method for using the Dark Night in a story where the lead can't change is to split the lead into two people. In this method, there is the protagonist, who doesn't change, and the main character, who does. Or, perhaps you reverse it, and the main character doesn't change but the protagonist does. Either way, you're shifting the change off onto another character and enjoying the benefits without the downside. So, the unchanging main character gains a co-lead/sidekick just for that story, and then that character transforms and finishes their character arc, and the lead has a new partner the next time.
- Gradual Change – In very long stories, like TV series with many seasons, or novel series, sometimes you spread the change out over a long three-act arc which spans the entire series. In any one particular story, the character doesn't change significantly, but over the course of the epic story they do. By presenting the change as a series of smaller changes, you get an unchanging

character who is changing, but doing it at a pace which lets them stay mostly the same in between stories.

The key is to think about your own particular needs as a storyteller, and what you need the character to do. Remember again that characters are there to serve the story, not the other way around, and set things up in whatever way works best for the story you're trying to tell. This is important to do at the planning stage, or else you might find you have a character the audience expects to change, but who you want to stay the same, or the reverse. Either way, consider at the start whether this structure is right for your story, because it doesn't work for everything.

And, it is also the Dark Night of the Soul where the American Three Act Structure and some other approaches go their separate ways. Any three-act structure stories can use the Dark Night of the Soul, but they don't have to, and often don't bother with it. Instead, the main character in some stories may start the story by realizing that they need to change (and this story is how they are changing, so there's no need for the Dark Night of the Soul because they had that at the beginning), or the main character learns the need to change in baby steps as they find themselves unable to overcome smaller challenges and must reflect and make small changes to keep moving forward.

In some ways, the latter approach is actually a more realistic structure, as human beings don't usually change overnight or after a single big dramatic life event, but in small increments. This slower pattern is also a natural fit for serialized fiction, where a character's journey is normally made up of a series of smaller stories and the character changes gradually over time. For example, Japanese manga creators avoid the version of the three-act structure beloved by Americans exactly because it doesn't work well with serialized stories. Spending many chapters on a character's descent into personal hell would only result in losing readers who would tire fast of a long series of defeats and downbeat chapters.

JAPANESE *KISHOTENKETSU* (SETS) STRUCTURE

The American Three-Act Structure is used by Americans and Western writers, but not all writers from all cultures take the same approach. One alternative that many storytellers find appealing is the Japanese *Kishotenketsu* structure (hereafter referred to as SETS Structure for reasons below), which is a storytelling structure that evolved from a style of Japanese poetry, but has been expanded to be used in many facets of modern Japanese storytelling from their 4-panel comic strips to film.

The SETS Structure consists of four phases, which correspond to the different syllables in the word *Kishotenketsu*, as you can see here:

- Ki – Setup (Introduction of the characters and situation)
- Sho – Events (Development of the situation presented in the setup)
- Ten – Twist (An unexpected (to the audience) dramatic event or turn occurs)
- Ketsu – Solution (The events resolve themselves in light of the Twist)

And here is a simple example of what this might look like in a typical four-panel comic form:

- Setup (Ki)- A man's dog is barking to go outside because there is a cat in their yard.
- Events (Sho) – The man lets the dog out and it runs straight at the cat.
- Twist (Ten) – The dog and cat begin to play happily together.
- Solution (Ketsu) – The tired dog comes back in and the cat leaves, both having had fun.

As you can see, it starts out with a normal situation, presents a twist on the audience's expectations (dogs usually hate cats), and then shows how it all resolves in the end. And, at first glance, it looks like a four-act story structure, but in reality it's only a typical three-act structure (setup-events (action)-solution) with a twist thrown in at the end of Act Two to surprise and create a dramatic question in the minds of the audience (what will happen next?).

However, what makes this structure really different is the way it handles the basic story unit- instead of being based around a conflict-centered action (someone trying to overcome something or beat something), the story unit here is about events simply happening in interesting ways. The drama here is occurring more in the minds of the audience than it is in the actual story. This is why SETS stories don't require a climax where everything comes together in a big dramatic way because there is no big final push to overcome opposition, just a natural ending that's the result of new or unexpected circumstances.

None of this means that a SETS structured story can't have conflict, or a dramatic climax, but the point here is that it doesn't have to- the conflict is optional. The Japanese use this structure to tell lots of stories with conflict, and most manga and anime are filled with conflict, even though they use this structure to one degree or another. But, it does offer an alternative way of thinking about the three-act structure and suggests ways in which story units can be presented that aren't so conflict or character driven. This is what allows the Japanese to master Slice of Life stories and offer some stories which have a calmer or more thoughtful tone than most western stories do. (In between the wild and over-the-top tone many manga take.)

SPEAR STRUCTURE – A SIMPLE FIVE-ACT STRUCTURE

The problem with the American Three-Act Structure is that it's a very specific way of telling stories, and one which doesn't work for all storytelling situations. For example, while it works fine as an overall structure for a story, it doesn't work well in individual chapters or scenes. You could try applying it to chapters or scenes in a story, and it might work in some cases, but not every chapter (or scene) is a complete story with rises and falls within it. Thus, the American Three-Act Structure isn't very scale-able.

At the same time, not all stories need to follow the particular flow that the American Three-Act Structure creates. For example, would you use this structure in writing three or four panel comic strips? Or, how about for writing long serial stories? There are cases where the American Three-Act Structure not only fails to work, but would get in the way if you tried to apply it religiously. This is probably one of the reasons that the Japanese don't use it in their prolific manga (comic book) storytelling industry or animation, because it doesn't suit what they're trying to do or how they tell stories.

Thus, a simpler structure is needed- one which is scalable, flexible, and allows for stories to be told that aren't locked into the morality play or heroic journey dynamic. At the same time, it needs to be a structure that works when telling stories which aren't just based on conflict, but just entertaining the audience and keeping them engaged while giving the writer a direction. The following structure, which is referred to by the acronym SPEAR is an attempt to create such a plot structure.

In short, the phases of SPEAR structure are as follows:

- Setup
- Problem
- (Interesting) Events
- Apex
- Resolution

These story elements might seem too simple to some readers, but their simplicity is their strength. Because they're so simple, these five story elements cover the five phases of any scene, chapter, story arc, episode, novel, or film. From the smallest unit (scene), to the largest (book, movie, series), you can break the story down into these five phases, and always know which story elements you're working toward next. Sometimes each of these five elements is a scene or chapter by itself, or sometimes only three or four of them are found in a particular scene. It doesn't matter, because as long as some of the parts are there, the story is moving forward.

Let's look at each of the phases of SPEAR structure in more detail, to understand exactly how they work.

Setup (First 10%)

In the Introduction phase, the writer needs to establish **who**'s involved, **where** they are, **when** this is happening, and (if needed) what their goal is, and why they're motivated to pursue it. Most (if not all) of these should be established as quickly as possible in any story or scene, and they can be established in any order.

Example:

Our main character is Hannah Tachibana, an aspiring Japanese-American Sushi Chef who returned to her father's birthplace on Hokkaido to study under her father's master. (Who, Where) Her dream is win the Musashi Cup, and prove that a half-Japanese woman can become a master sushi chef. (Motivation, Goal- Attain)

In Chapter 62 of Hannah's story, she has finally won the approval from her tough master to open her own restaurant, and wants to have a big opening day event to prove she's ready to enter the restaurant world.

Problem (Next 15%)

Once the audience knows who's involved in the story, then the writer needs to establish what problem the character is trying to overcome. Problems can come in many forms, but the thing they all have in common is that they give the character something to do. Without a problem to overcome there would be no story, because the character would just be sitting there playing games on their phone and relaxing. A problem is someone or something which is standing in the way of the character achieving their goals, whatever those are.

- If a character is trying to get a high grade, then passing a test can be a problem.
- If a character is trying to rescue a prince, then getting past a dragon is a problem.
- If a character is trying to take a nap, then a friend who keeps texting them is a problem.

- If a character is trying to survive, then a country is falling into anarchy is a problem.

The character has a goal (even if it's just relaxing), and the problem is preventing that from happening, so the character needs to do something about it.

Two other things which happen during the Problem phase are the establishment of Plot Points, and the introduction of any Opposition.

Plot Points

After the Setup phase, the Problem phase is the last chance the writer has to set up all of the significant plot elements of the story that are going to play out in the remaining three phases. If something isn't introduced (or at least hinted at) by the end of the Problem phase, it is going to come out of nowhere and make the reader unhappy. The potential for things to happen and the setup for all the Interesting Events which follow must be done before the Problem phase ends. Whether that's establishing story elements of the setting to be used later, showing character traits, introducing opponents, or anything else that needs to happen to explain why the rest of the story plays out the way it does, it happens here.

For example, if you're going to have it rain at the end, the storm clouds better be gathering on the horizon by now. If your character is going to suddenly speak Chinese later, you need to at least hint at that ability by now. If there's going to be a shooting at the climax, that gun had better be on the mantle place waiting before the Problem phase ends.

Opposition

During the Problem phase, we'll also learn about the potential obstacles the character faces in achieving their goals (if we haven't already been introduced to them in the Introduction) that will be coming up during the Interesting Events phase. Just like Plot Points, some or most of the Opposition they will face should be set up or hinted at by the Problem phase, with it becoming an actual problem during the Interesting Events phase. If a goal can be met without opposition, it usually isn't worth telling a story about. In fact, often the heart of a story isn't the character's goal or action being taken to meet that goal, it's the challenges that come with reaching that goal. If there's no opposition to the character's actions, then the story moves to the Ending phase.

Opposition can come in any form that prevents the character from achieving their goals; however, these too tend to fall into one of several categories:

- Active Opposition.
- Passive Opposition.

- Lack of resources.
- Lack of ability.

Active Opposition– an opponent who is actively trying to prevent the character from achieving their goal. Usually they have the same (or similar) goal as the main character, and this common goal brings them into direct opposition with each other.

Passive Opposition– an opponent who stands in the way of the character achieving their goals, but who isn't pursuing the same goal as the main character. They are pursuing their own goals, but because of their existence/presence it prevents the main character from achieving their goal.

Lack of Resources– the character has a goal, but lacks the physical resources (time, money, friends, contacts, clothes, equipment, etc.) to achieve that goal. This will usually require the character to pursue other smaller goals first (like getting a job to earn money) to achieve their goal.

Lack of Ability– the character has a goal, but lacks the personal skills, requirements, or knowledge needed to reach that goal. This can most often be solved through training and personal improvement, or occasionally by finding someone else who has the abilities needed and getting them to do it.

Remember too that a single story can have more than one obstacle to a single goal. Just as there can be big goals and little goals, there can be big obstacles and little obstacles as well, and often the character needs to accomplish several little goals first to be able to accomplish the big final goal.

Example:
Hannah Tachibana rents a new restaurant space, gets it all set up, and puts out flyers advertising her new opening day. On the day of the grand opening, she holds up a can of her favorite saké and tells her servers and workers that she will toast it with them at the end of the day when they've given their all and had a successful opening day. (Plot Point, Goal) Then they start getting ready, and everything seems to be going well, but...

Interesting Events (50%)

The Interesting Events phase is where entertaining things happen as the character tries to pursue their goals. Interesting Events (Events for short) can be almost anything, as long as they meet two requirements:

1. Are interesting and/or entertaining to the audience.
2. Are connected with the story's Spine of Action.

As long as the Event meets these two criteria, it's an Event. Whether it's a character meeting another interesting person, a character breaking out in song, or a duel to the death- these are all possible events just so long as they're interesting/entertaining and they're linked in some way to the central spine of action of the story.

Here is a list of a few possible Interesting Events the author can use to interest or entertain the audience:

- Introducing new characters
- Introducing new situations
- Introducing challenges to the character's goals
- Creative solutions to challenges
- Conflict with other characters
- Revealing new details about characters
- Offering new perspectives
- Offering relevant new ideas
- Twists and turns in the plot
- A surprising/unexpected reaction to an event.
- A surprising explanation for something which already happened.
- Presenting interesting imagery
- Offering beautiful prose/art
- Introducing surprising/interesting facts
- New takes on old ideas
- Teaching the audience something they didn't know
- Teaching the audience how to do something new
- Giving an interesting and relevant quote
- Presenting a philosophical question
- Having something funny happen
- Having something scary happen
- Having something sexy happen
- Having something tragic happen
- Having something unexpected happen
- Telling the audience a relevant joke

Any of these can be an Event in a story- something which keeps the audience's attention and makes them entertained. Also, you might notice the word "relevant" pops up a few times in that list, that's a reminder that every Interesting Event which happens must be connected with the story and situation in which it's happening. For example, a powerful quote like "To strive, to seek, to find, and not to yield!" is great to have someone say in a situation where the character is facing a crisis of confidence and wants to give up. However, if the situation is about buying milk and bread at the grocery story, it's going to be a little out of place. (Unless the goal is to show the character is off their meds that day.)

Let's look at two examples of Interesting Events in action:

- Setup: A witch is home bored one day.
- Problem: Her house is dirty, so she decides to clean her house. (Spine of Action: Cleaning house.)
- Event: She has her black cat familiar transform into a handsome singer to provide music.
- Event: She orders her furniture to march outside and shake off the dust, which it does.
- Event: She summons up some skeletons to take her clothes out and wash them while she dances to the cat's singing.
- Event: In the pantry, she has house goblins wash the dishes while she drinks tea.
- Apex: When it's all done, she flops down on the couch and curls up with her cat for a nap.
- Resolution: Cleaning is so hard, she moans while the skeletons and house goblins collapse in exhaustion around her.

As you can see, in this example the Interesting Events happening all meet the basic two criteria- They're interesting, and they're connected with the Spine of Action of the story. You might also notice that they don't involve conflict, and this is important to understand (especially for North Americans raised on conflict-driven stories)- <u>not all stories or story events require conflict</u>. Conflict is powerful tool for making audiences interested, but it's just one type of interesting situation that the characters can face in the story, it's not the ONLY one.

In the above story, the things happening to the witch are interesting (to the audience), but she faces no actual challenges as she tries to accomplish her goals. The interesting parts of the story are seeing how she accomplishes her tasks in interesting and magical ways, not how she overcomes some great challenges and find solutions. That would be fine too, but it's not the only entertaining way to tell the story, and the important part in storytelling is that the audience is kept entertained- everything else is secondary.

Let's look at another example:

- Setup: A witch is home bored one day.
- Problem: Her wizard boyfriend calls and says he's coming over to talk about something important. She's overjoyed, thinking he's going to ask her to marry him, until she realizes her house is a mess and worries he'll change his mind if he sees it. (Spine of Action: Cleaning house to impress boyfriend, fast!)
- Event: Problem- the furniture is dusty, Solution- she animates it to run outside and shake.
- Event: Problem- the kitchen is a mess, Solution- she summons house goblins to clean it.
- Apex: Problem- the floor needs cleaning, Bigger problem- she's running low on magic because she used it to animate the furniture and summon the goblins, Solution- she grabs a broom and goes to work as fast as she can.
- Resolution: The doorbell rings, and she rushes to the door, using the last of her magic to change her messy appearance at the last second to clean herself up. She opens the door, and he's there with a limo to take her out to lunch. He never enters the house. Later, as he tries to propose marriage, she's fallen asleep from exhaustion and misses her big chance.

This is roughly the same story, but now it is more conflict based. It's about her overcoming a series of problems which stand in the way of her accomplishing her goal(s). It has a clear Spine of Action (preparing for the big moment), problems to be overcome that will make the audience think how they'd handle things (and be amused at seeing how a witch does it), escalating tension, and finally an amusing twist at the end which is the unexpected result of everything that happened in trying to achieve the main character's goals.

However, since conflict-based situations are often the heart of many stories, here is a list of the few more common types of challenging Interesting Events characters might face:

- **Mental**- The character doesn't have the skills or knowledge to overcome the issue.
- **Social**- The character can't do something without affecting their place in society or the community, or with friends, or with family.
- **Emotional**- Something the character isn't emotionally able to deal with or accept.
- **Physical**- Something that literally stands in the way of the character achieving their goal.

- **Financial**- Gaining or losing money or resources.
- **Legal**- Issues related to law, rules, or contracts which prevent or limit the character's actions.
- **Spiritual**- Issues based on spiritual beliefs or religious law which prevent or limit a character's actions.
- **Practical**- Whether the character has the ability or resources to take action.
- **Technical**- Problems related to computers or technology and the limits of that technology.
- **Ethical**- Things that run up against the character's personal beliefs, code of conduct, or honor.
- **Philosophical**- Based on ideas of life, existence, human nature, values, etc.
- **Essential**- Events based on basic human needs (food, sleep, sex, etc.) not being fulfilled.
- **Procedural**- Problems that happen when trying to follow a procedure.

Examples:
It's opening day at Hannah Tachibana's restaurant, but...

- **Mental**- She realizes her food preparation plans are wrong and needs to fix them. So, Hannah delegates the food preparation to her sous chef and retreats to her office to re-plan the menu.
- **Social**- She realizes she forgot to ask permission from the local restaurant owner's association to set up her restaurant, and now they're threatening to blacklist her. So, Hannah has her friend deliver a fine bottle of whisky and a letter of apology to the local restaurant association head and offers him a free dinner at the opening.
- **Emotional**- She has a panic attack and isn't sure she can cook, so Hannah calls her Dad to help her overcome her panic.
- **Physical**- There is a leak in the unit above her restaurant and the ceiling tiles fall down, ruining the decorations. So, Hannah calls a plumber to fix the leak, borrows some ceiling tiles temporarily from an unused extra room, and has her assistants string up new decorations.
- **Financial**- She discovers she doesn't have enough money for the fish delivery man who only accepts cash. So, Hannah borrows money from her assistants to pay for the fish.
- **Legal**- She discovers she didn't get a license to serve alcohol, but sake is part of main course. So, Hannah decides that tonight will be alcohol free, and serves a chilled fruit vinegar instead.

- **Spiritual**- She remembers that the guests she invited can't eat her main dish for religious reasons. So, Hannah gets her sous-chef to cover for her while she quickly whips up an extra dish just for that table.
- **Practical**- She discovers that she can't prepare fast enough for the number of people who show up. So, Hannah sends out free appetizers to the tables who will have to wait and apologizes to them for the delays.
- **Technical**- She discovers her cash register isn't working properly. So, Hannah quietly sends an assistant to ask a neighbor if he could take a look at it.
- **Ethical**- She discovers she bought the wrong kind of Tuna, and must decide whether to serve it or not. So, Hannah innovates and calls the Tuna "Rocket Tuna" and cooks it with a blowtorch before it goes out to cover the texture issues.
- **Philosophical**- She believes every customer must be happy, but one customer sends everything back. So, Hannah grabs a cart and goes out to personally prepare a dish for them tableside in an effort to make them happy.
- **Essential**- She's running out of energy and can't keep up. She has her assistant make a run to the story for energy drinks to keep her going.
- **Procedural**- She discovers she is missing a key component of her main dish. So, Hannah hops on her Motorcycle and drives as fast as she can to the nearest fish market to get some.

Avoid big Events which weren't set up in some way in the Problem phase, and major Events should be chosen carefully and with consideration for how they will affect both the story and the character. Too many big Interesting Events can slow the story down, and, of course, the important thing is- how does this Event reflect the core idea(s) or theme(s) of your story?

Audience vs. Character

Once the Interesting Events phase starts, the main character will encounter their first dramatic event- something which produces a reaction from the character and/or audience. This can come in the form of problems, challenges, surprises, obstacles, reveals, plot twists, and is where the "interesting" part of the story happens.

There are two basic kinds of Events- those that affect the characters and those that affect the audience. Character Events (like encountering opposition, succeeding, or failing) are things which cause the characters to feel emotions, and Audience Events (like interesting situations, imagery, reveals and plot twists) are ones which cause the audience to feel emotions. Often, Events affect both the characters and the audience, but not always, or in the same way.

For example, a character might think a series of Events like finding a winning lottery ticket and meeting a new girlfriend are good things, while the audience knows they are both part of a scam and feels anxious as they see the character falling deeper and deeper into a trap. Or perhaps a character is asked a question which they think nothing of, but the audience recognizes that the character is actually making a choice which will result in a life or death situation. In both of these Events, the character's reaction is separate from that of the audience.

The thing to remember here is that while Interesting Events which cause the character to feel will generally cause the audience to feel, the reverse is obviously not true. Just because the audience feels something doesn't mean the character will, unless the story is some form of interactive experience like a game where the audience can make choices that directly affect the character's choices. So, when we're talking about Events in this section, we're talking mostly about Events which affect the character, but it should be assumed anything that affects the character also affects the audience as well.

Thus, Interesting Events are built around one simple rule – they must make the audience have a reaction.

That reaction might be wonder, heartbreak, lust, shock, horror, disgust, curiosity, or any of the many other human emotions or reactions, but an Interesting Event must make them react to be considered an Event. It doesn't matter whether the Event is good, or bad, or neutral, they must always be something that will engage the audience in some way, if it doesn't, it's not an Event.

The most basic feeling for an Event to generate is interest or curiosity, and most Interesting Events in a story create some form of these emotions because that's how the storyteller keeps the audience involved. This is where the concept of Dramatic Questions (see *Controlling Ideas*: Engagement) comes from, as they are the specific questions the Events that happen create in the minds of the audience and which keep the audience involved in the story.

The next most common feeling writers try to evoke in their audience is shock or surprise, which are usually produced by showing or revealing things that that audience doesn't expect. This is where dramatic twists come into play, and those Events which take the story in a different direction or show previous Events in a new light. These are so common that audiences now expect at least one twist or revelation somewhere in most stories to keep the story lively and interesting. Whether you give it to them, of course, is up to you.

After this comes the wide range of other human emotions, from love to hate, anger to peacefulness, disappointment to triumph- Interesting Events in stories can make the audience feel all of these feelings and more. As the main character experiences these things, so will the audience riding alongside them, and as the Events play out in different ways the audience's own emotions will be carried along in a tide of feeling.

The key here is to remember that Events are there to make the audience react in some way, and even the emotions of the characters are there to direct the feelings of the audience. A story is an emotional experience as much as it is an intellectual one, and you are there to take your readers for a ride.

Many people think Events should only be negative, with the writer throwing lots of challenges at the main character, but you could also have a story where nothing but good things happen to the main character- as long as those Events are fascinating to the reader it doesn't matter. Events often create questions and answer questions and do it in the most exciting ways possible. Each Event could make the reader ask a Dramatic Question- usually involving one of the key questions words- who, what, where, when, why, or how.

While there might just be one Event in a story, depending on the length of the story, there may be dozens, or even hundreds, of Events which happen. Also, Events come in all sizes, and sometimes there are many smaller Events instead of a single big one (or several big ones). Usually, however, there is a series of ever-bigger Events which lead up to a big final one which usually occurs during the Climax phase.

Event Patterns

As a general rule, Interesting Events usually get more intense as the story (or scene) plays out, with each one trying to top the previous one for entertainment or interest value. Like any entertainment act, Events should start small, and build, giving the reader a sense that they're moving towards a big finish. At the same time, however, there needs to be ebbs and flows, where each Event is followed by a brief pause before the next bigger event is introduced.

In the second example above, the problem/solution format creates this ebb and flow effect by having the "problem" being introduced as the slow moment while the "solution" is the big interesting event which interests or amuses the reader. This back and forth, sine-wave pattern, is what keeps the audience from getting overloaded with constant stimulation by giving them a brief break before the story moves on to the next Event. If you pay attention, you can find this "ebb and flow" effect being used in most stories and music, where the best artists are masters of balancing fast and slow in a way which carries their audiences up without overloading them. In music, they alternate between vocals, instrumentals, fast tempo parts, slow tempo parts, different instruments and musical styles to keep the audience interested and wondering what will happen next.

Writing a story is no different.

Thinking about Events

Here is a list of questions to ask yourself as you plan your Events:

- How will this Event make my audience react?

- Is this an audience centered Event or a character centered one?
- How does this Event help or hurt my character's Problem?
- How will this Event or its resolution reflect my story's central themes and/or argument(s)?
- How much time will this Event take to play out? Do I have enough space or time to tell it properly?
- Is there another Event (or type of Event) which would work better for my story?
- Do I have too many Events? Am I giving my audience time to breath?
- How will this Event affect my story's pacing?
- How will this Event affect my story's tension level?
- Is this Event raising or lowering the tension and drama level of the story? How does it compare with the Events before and after it?

Final Thoughts

Another thing to consider is what the focus of your story is- setting, character, or plot. That focus will determine where most of your Interesting Events are coming from. For example, if your story is setting based, then the majority of Events should be a natural result of the rules and nature of the setting itself. (So, if your characters are on a volcanic island, lava flows and eruptions might be natural Events to occur. Or if your story is about dog breeders, then the Events will relate to the issues and challenges that come with breeding dogs.) On the other hand, if your story is character based, then almost all your Events should come from the decisions and choices made by characters within the story, primarily your main character. (This usually requires the character to make a choice, and the Event is happening because of that choice, even if that choice was to make no decision at all.) And finally, in a plot-based story, the Events can really come from anywhere, and may include more Events which are random, co-incidences, or just plain bad luck. (Although it's best to still make them connected with the setting and characters when you can.)

To conclude, remember that Interesting Events tend to naturally create more Interesting Events, so be on the lookout for more Events which are the natural side-effect of ones which already happened. In martial arts stories, for example, defeating one opponent puts you in bad blood with his friends and allies, who are then likely going to come looking for you. Murphy's Law is strongly in effect in stories, and usually the worst thing that can happen, will happen. (Because that's much more entertaining and dramatic than good things happening.) Just make a point of thinking your stories through logically, and thinking about what would naturally happen next and the possible consequences of what characters do. If you do this, you'll quickly find you'll be trying to cut down the number of Events not come up with more!

Apex (20%)

When your story built up to its fever pitch, and it's time for the main character to pull the fat out of the fire, it's time to move into the Apex phase.

This is the point where all the dramatic elements of the story come together. Often, the main character must make their final and most tough decisions, and it's the point that everything in the story is leading up to. At that point, the main character will either succeed or fail based on their choices, and we will know the results. This is the moment the audience has been waiting for since they started this journey, so give the audience their big finale and get ready to wrap things up.

Example:

Hannah Tachibana has faced a series of crises surrounding her opening day, but through staying calm and using the training her master gave her in restaurant management, she's able to solve all the problems and her grand opening is a success.

Resolution (Last 5%)

The Resolution phase is there to show what happens after the main character wins (or rarely, loses), and is where the character receives their rewards for what they did in the story. This is where you bring it all together and show how all that hard work paid off. The character gets the love interest, respect, money, or whatever else you want to give them to show the audience that this was the right way to go about things and that this way should be rewarded. This can be a single panel shot in a comic, or it can be several whole chapters in a book, either way, it's a needed part of the story.

The important thing you need to remember about the end of a story is that it should always feel natural based on the events which occurred in the story. Everything in a story is about setup and payoff, and nothing should happen that was not set up in some way previously, including the end of the story itself. One great way to make sure this happens is to not only know what the point of the story is, but also plan the ending first and write toward that ending. All story thematic arguments have a natural ending, and you just need to figure out how that argument's conclusion is represented in your story.

Example:

The chapter ends with Hannah's workers discussing how well things went, and then turning around to find Hannah flopped out in a chair asleep with her hat over her face. One of them puts something in her hand and then they quietly leave. When the server is asked what he left with her, we get a shot of her clutching that can of saké she'd been planning to toast with at the end of the night and a smile on the sleeping Hannah's face.

Keep it Simple

Reading through all the above, you might find yourself a little overwhelmed. There's quite a bit of detail there, and each of the four SPEAR stages has a surprising amount of smaller parts within it. However, the truth is most of that detail is just there to make it clear what usually goes where, but you don't need to constantly remember or refer back to it. All you need to remember is the core concept of the SPEAR structure.

If it helps, just convert SPEAR structure into basic 3-Act Structure and you're good to go.

- Act 1 (25%)- Situation and Problem
- Act 2 (50%)- Interesting Events
- Act 3 (25%)- Apex and Resolution

See? Not that complicated. Just remember the fundamentals, and you'll do fine. If you need to know precisely what to put in each part, the above detailed version will cover your needs, but otherwise just remember the basics and it'll all be okay.

Story Length

This SPEAR structure will work for everything from individual scenes, to chapters, to story arcs, to novels, to whatever else you want to write. It's based on the very basic building blocks of storytelling, and so almost all stories of any length will follow some version of it.

You might have noticed that there are percentages attached to each phase of the story (10%, 15%, 50%, 20%, and 5% respectively) and wondered how set in stone those are. The answer is they're not set in stone at all, and are general numbers based on how modern stories usually run and how most stories are set up. Most stories have a fast opening, quick buildup, lots of action, and then a quick close to bring everything home at the end. However, if you want to play with them, and make them different lengths, go right ahead! If you want to do something more character driven or slower you might want to use a formula more like 20%, 30%, 35%, 5%, 10% or maybe you want something faster and want to make it 5%, 10%, 60%, 20%, 5%. Whatever works for you and the story you're trying to tell is fine.

The main reason those percentages are there is to act as a planning guide, for which they are extremely useful, especially when scripting. So, if you have 30 pages to work with for your story or chapter, you know that Pages 1-3 are going to be for the

Setup, Pages 4-8 are for Problem, Pages 9-22 are there for Interesting Events, Pages 23-28 are the big climax at the Apex, and Pages 29+30 are for the Resolution. You can even develop your own versions of this pattern with more details at certain points, like for example saying you'll usually put your Apex at the 90% mark and only give yourself Page 27-29 to wrap it on up.

Flexibility

SPEAR plot structure is also super flexible, and can be shaped as the writer wishes. If you want to delay some part of it, or re-arrange something to suit your story, you can! For example, when used in chapters in a larger story, the structure used in middle chapters is often SPEA or RSPEA instead of SPEAR. In other words, each middle chapter begins by telling the results of the Apex (or at least the Resolution) of the previous chapter, then introduces the new situation, problem, and characters, develops them, and begins a new series of Interesting Events with an Apex left unresolved (or semi-resolved) for the next chapter. Some writers also like to start with an Interesting Event and then jump around in time (ESPEAR) and some writers might even start with the ending and explain how it all came about (RSPEA). Again, the sky is the limit and the only boundaries are the writer's creativity.

FINAL THOUGHTS ON PLOT AS STORY STRUCTURE

Presented here were three versions of the three-act structure, but the Internet is filled with many different variations. Many of them are there to add more detail, or place emphasis on certain parts of the story to go along with a particular genre or style of writing. You can find some of the more notable ones under the Story/Plotting Formulas tab at robynpaterson.com, which range from a "12-Chapter Murder Mystery Formula" to links to Kat O'keeffe's video where she breaks the 3 acts down into 9 phases each for 27 "chapters".

Don't be afraid to experiment, and try new things, because there is no perfect version of the three-act structure out there, just different attempts to use it in new and interesting ways. Also, check out the Storytelling Writing and Tactics section for more thoughts on how to apply story structure to make your writing soar.

SETTING

There are two mistakes people tend to make when they think of the setting of a story.

The first is that when most people hear the word "setting," they commonly associate it with answers to questions starting with "where." Where does the story take place? Where does the scene happen? Where are the characters from? Where did she keep that gun?

In other words, they think it's talking about a place.

However, the setting of a story covers a lot more than just geography. It also covers the whole world in which the characters live, from the structures, to the cultures, to the languages, the people, the weather, the time period, the food, the magic, and everything in between. Setting in story, then, actually refers to everything in the story which is not the main characters.

The second mistake people make is that they think of settings, especially ones which are set in present day locations, as being real. They are most certainly not. Like characters, and pretty much everything else in a story, the setting of a story is a creation of fiction, a place which exists to act as a location for the story and events to play out. It might be based on a real place, it might feel like a real place with astounding detail, but it is no more real than a movie set or a theatre backdrop. Whether you're immersing yourself in attending Hogwarts, voyaging in the final frontier, wandering Paris with Le Comte in the 1830's, or standing in present day New York City, unless you're really at those times and places physically yourself, you're experiencing a fictional recreation.

This is something you should consider freeing. Liberating.

If all places in fiction are fake, and everything in them as well, then the writer is free to do whatever they want with them. If you want to make it snow in June in Texas, or have them serve poutine in Tokyo, or say the sidewalks in Nairobi are blue- in your world, they are. You're not limited by reality, and can play with all the elements of the world around your characters in your story as much or as little as you want to achieve whatever effect you want. You can have people behave the way you want, have them speak the way you want, and have them express or represent any views or ideas you want.

You are a god when creating stories, and the reality within them reflects your idea of reality, not the way it really is. So, go nuts! Have fun! Don't worry about the details! Just get your ideas onto the page and have the world in the story express the world you want the audience to hear, see, feel, taste and experience.

However, there are a few small catches.

As when we talked about how characters must be acceptable, consistent and consistently inconsistent, the same rules also apply to the setting of a story.

To begin with, the audience must be willing to accept the world you're showing them, and the more your presentation of the world differs from the reality they know, the less willing they'll be to believe in it. So, if you start making up street names or locations for New York city, people who know the real NYC are going to have a hard time accepting that as a real place. Likewise, if you have the laws of gravity work differently, or go against the world that the audience knows or is ready to accept, then they'll have trouble immersing themselves in it because they'll be too busy thinking about all the things that are wrong with it.

But, before you panic and open up thirty tabs worth of research for your next story set in NYC, calm down a moment and keep reading. Firstly, that will only apply to people who actually know the place well, and secondly, the audience knows this is fiction, so they're willing to give you a little room to play. As long as you don't make any major changes to the reality they know without being willing to explain those changes, they'll go with it. So, if you say that animal-themed pantsuits are all the rage this year in NYC due to popular movie sparking a craze, then the audience will just accept that such an event could happen and keep reading. This is fiction, and audience will be perfectly willing to let you play with reality as long as you follow the other two rules.

The next rule is that you must be consistent, which when we're talking about fiction simply means that once you've established something is true, it must always be true. So, if animal-themed pantsuits are the rage this year in NYC in your reality, then that must continue to be true for however long the story needs it to be. If magic works, if people live alongside dinosaurs, or if we're on the planet Quent, it doesn't matter so long as once you establish something and get the audience to accept it, you're consistent with it. You set the stage, you tell the audience the rules, and you stick with them.

And, if you need to break those rules, it better be for something that is not only important, but also something which you're ready to explain to the audience because you need to be consistently inconsistent. In other words, if there are any inconsistencies, they'd better be there for a reason, and they'd better be explained, or the audience is going to lose faith in your ability to construct a believable and acceptable world.

So, to sum up, when building the world around your characters, you need to create an acceptable, consistent, and consistently inconsistent place.

And, here are a few more tips.

The more you change reality, the more you have to explain. Therefore, one good approach is to only change as much as you need to for the purposes of your story and setting, and no more. If you need there to be a school at a certain place and there isn't, then change it and don't worry about it because only a small number of local readers will notice, and most won't care. If you want to add mutant superpowers to your setting, add them, and then try to keep the rest of the setting as close to our reality as you can while still being logically consistent. The more new material readers need to learn, the more it slows down the telling of your story. (Unless, of course, the setting material is the point the story.)

Also, whenever possible, try to base your setting off reality in some fashion. It's less things the audience needs to learn, and it will make it easier for them to get up to speed. This is one of the reasons why most fantasy settings look and work vaguely like medieval Europe, because it gives the audience a premade real-world template to work from. However, just remember one of science fiction writer Larry Niven's rules of writing: "The bigger the lie, the sooner you tell it." In other words, if there's a major change from our reality in the story, tell that to the audience as soon as you possibly can, even on page one of a book. If everyone in your setting are talking fish people, you let the audience know right away, the same with if your story takes place on a space station, or there's magic in the modern world. (Unless, as usual, it's part of the story that it's a surprise.)

Different genres also have different settings conventions and tropes, so be aware of the ones which apply to your story. This is doubly true for the more speculative genres like science fiction and fantasy where you're often building whole worlds. For example, it's expected by audiences that you have faster-than-light drives of some kind in a space opera setting, so you don't need to take time to explain them (unless you want to, or it's connected with the plot) and can just casually mention their use and go on with the story as if it isn't important. The same with magic in a fantasy setting, once you establish its presence you only need to explain the most basic of details about it unless it's really powerful or a plot point. This is also why in the DC Universe, Superman can put on a pair of glasses and turn into a normal guy who nobody recognizes- it's a genre convention, everyone just accepts it and goes with it.

One note for those of you who love worldbuilding- most readers don't care about your amazing setting except as it pertains to the story being told. So, if you have lots of setting-based information you want them to know, space it out over the story and only tell them what they need to know at the time to understand and follow the story. Think of it as coating the harder to swallow bits in chocolate- you can get people to eat almost anything small covered in chocolate, but if you try to get them to eat something larger they'll gag, no matter how sweet you make it. We don't call it "world dumping" for a reason, you don't dump it all on the audience at once.

Finally, if you need to make really extreme changes, it's often easier to create a new setting than to try to modify an existing one. For example, many young adult novels are set in post-apocalyptic settings because it's much easier to literally wipe the civilization slate clean and rebuild than try to set the stories in fictional modern places. (Also, audiences are pretty accepting of civilizations collapsing because they do all the time in reality.) Jumping forward in time is also useful, and you can explain away social changes through past events to sharpen and define the key elements of the setting you want to focus on.

THE POWER OF LIMITED LOCATIONS

Many people who enjoy writing science fiction and fantasy love building worlds, and they can't wait to show those worlds off to their audience in glorious detail. However, just as you need to limit the number of characters in a story to avoid confusing your audience, you also need to limit the number of locations to as few as you can get away with. This might seem counter-intuitive, since after all, you're sometimes building a whole world in your story setting, but just like many things in stories the setting where the drama happens is actually something small that represents a larger whole.

So, for example, let's says you had a story which is about the struggles of different social classes in a bustling port city. Naturally, you want to show the audience how the lives of the people in different social classes vary from each other. However, you can't show the whole city and everywhere in it, so instead you need to break the setting down into a limited number of locations where each represents a piece of the greater whole for the audience to see.

The run-down apartment of a dock worker in a poor immigrant neighborhood, the middle-class suburban house of a manager, an upscale penthouse in an elite district where a rich family lives, and a factory where the rich owners, managers, and poor workers interact would be all you'd need to let the audience see how the different classes of this city live. Four different locations, but together they'd provide the key information the audience needs to understand the situations and circumstances of the people in the story.

A few carefully picked highly detailed locations where the audience can feel a living, breathing setting are worth a hundred sparsely detailed randomly chosen ones.

The audience knows that each of your story locations is (or should be) symbolic of the greater world they can't see, and will naturally try to fill in the gaps with their own ideas and imaginations based on the information you give them.

This is the same imaginative power that lets playwrights transform a few dozen square meters of stage into anywhere in space and time with just a few costumes and props, and is a power you can utilize in your own stories to bring your worlds to life. You just need to give the audience the key details to send their imaginations in the right direction, and they'll do the rest.

THE ARENA PRINCIPAL

Another important reason for limiting the number of locations in your story is what could be called the Arena Principal- the less space your characters have to move around in, the more interactions they will have, and the more drama that can occur.

Stories are based on dramatic interactions between characters, and drama happens when characters who are in conflict or don't like each other are kept in close proximity to each other. Whether it's a single room, a house, a small town, a city neighborhood, a farm, or a spaceship, the characters need to be able to interact with each other and often be forced to interact because of the circumstances of the story.

Characters are like sticks: on their own they can only sit there, but if you rub two of them together right- bang! Fire! And this interaction between characters is what will give your story the dramatic energy you need to keep the story interesting and keep the drama going. So, you need to make sure that they can't easily escape or avoid each other because if they can, they naturally would, and you'll have no drama, and possibly no story.

In practical terms, this means always answering a single question- "Why don't they just leave?"

This is a question that's always going to be in the heads of your audience, and you need to answer it. Whether you give emotional reasons (feeling lazy), social reasons (not wanting to look like a coward), physical reasons (too far to walk), financial reasons (can't afford a ticket), or technical reasons (the car's broken), there should always be a reason why the characters are staying in a situation they don't want to be in.

Now, they might be trying to get out, but that's drama, so that's okay. (As long as it fits your story.)

So, when you're planning stories, think like a Roman emperor!

Cut off their escape routes, herd them into interesting locations, and let them do battle for the amusement of the masses!

That's the Arena Principal.

That's entertainment!

SETTING AND CHARACTER

Something writers should always think about when planning a story is whether their characters and setting are in sync or not. If the character and the setting are in sync, then the character is in a setting where they belong and are a part of that setting. On the other hand, if the character and setting are not in sync with each other, then the character doesn't belong in that setting and is not a natural part of it.

This is important to think about from a storytelling point of view because it determines a lot of the focus of the story. If the character is in sync with the setting, then they are there to be our guides to the settings they inhabit, and often represent it in some way. For example, if our main character is a police detective living his daily grind, he's giving us a tour of the world a police detective lives in, and represents how that world shapes a police detective's personality, character, and life. In this case, a lot of the reader's information about the setting is coming from the character, and there doesn't need to be as much time spent explaining about the setting to the reader by the writer.

On the other hand, a powerful storytelling device is to have a character who isn't in sync with their setting in some way. At its most extreme you get *Alice in Wonderland*, where you have a normal character from our world in a setting which is nothing like ours, and by contrasting Alice and Wonderland, we see just how bizarre a place Wonderland really is. However, most stories which want to explore their settings take a lighter touch, and just have the character be different from the setting in smaller ways which serve the story.

Having an out of sync character is so powerful because it really lets you highlight certain elements of your setting. Whatever parts of the setting the character is out of sync with naturally become highlighted in the story and the minds of the reader, and end up under the magnifying glass. So, if the character is a bookworm surrounded by non-readers, then that becomes the focus of the story. Or, if the character is a thoughtful person surrounded by callous people, then that becomes a major part of the story. Anything you make out of sync between the character and setting, whether it's a tiny difference or a whole world, becomes the thing the story is about.

So, how does your main character reflect or not reflect the setting, and why?

Not thinking about this is ignoring a powerful tool in your writer's toolkit.

SETTING AND CONTROLLING IDEAS

So, since settings aren't real, how should they be built?

There are different ways to do it, but one strong way is to build them specifically to reflect the ideas being represented in the story. Like the characters, who also reflect those ideas, the setting is a world which has been custom created to show off and highlight the ideas of the story. For example, if your story is about class warfare, you could set it in modern day, or you could set it aboard a post-apocalyptic train where the closer you are to the front the higher your status is. (*Snowpiercer*) Or, if you're doing a story about injustice, you could set it during the French revolution when justice could change by the day or a man's whim. (*Les Misérables.*)

The point here is the setting is there to serve the story and the ideas the story is being used to convey, and shouldn't just be randomly picked, but instead be carefully chosen and modified to highlight the key points the story is trying to make. It doesn't have to be a fantastic setting either- you can make small changes to "real" places that will make them reflect certain ideas. The same inner-city street could reflect a story of hope or hopelessness, tragedy or triumph, the human spirit, or the depths of human depravity, all by making small changes to the setting and focusing on different aspects of it.

One other way settings and ideas come together is when you have a setting-driven story. This is when you use an existing real-world setting, culture, or activity to shape the stories and characters. This would be a story where the setting is the most important part of the story, and your story is about the characters changing under the pressures of the setting itself. In these kinds of stories, the setting is normally a real one, but the characters are fictional and chosen so that they reflect the different aspects of the setting and highlight the setting through their actions. One example of this would be some of the many stories written about the Salem Witch Trials, most of which are about characters who have normal lives that are torn apart and reshaped by those terrible events. Not that this technique is only about tragedies- stories where a character learns to master a sport like golf or to play chess and enters those sport subcultures can also be setting-based if the focus is on the activity and culture, not the character themselves.

SETTING AND PLOT

The setting of a story is often a crucial part of what happens in it.

The setting of a story determines what is possible and not possible in a story, and acts as framework that both enables the writer to do what they do, and the audience to understand what is happening based on context and situations. Most story events which don't rise out of the character's own actions will come from the setting around them, and the setting can be both a prison and a library for the writer- trapping them in a limited space where they can't move, or filling them with the freedom of imagination and ideas.

As was mentioned in the discussion of plot, almost everything that happens in a story should be set up by some element of the character or setting, and when it comes to setup, setting is king. Most of the events which play out in the story will be the result of characters interacting with setting in some way, and so setting acts as the spring from which all story events flow. Look back at the list of common types of events you see in stories, and you will see that the majority of them are external to the character or the result of character and setting coming into conflict.

This is why knowing your setting is so important, and whether you want to plan only the very roughest sketch of a setting, or a finely detailed recreation, you need to take the setting of a story seriously enough to look at it just like you do a major character. Perhaps more so because if it's based on a real place you'll need to be presenting details which are a natural part of that setting in real life. But, it's not all about just doing factual research, as the more you know about the setting the more ideas it will naturally generate for you.

For example, say a story is set in ancient China. If you know a bit about ancient China like their clothing, food, political system and social classes, that's probably enough to get by and gives you something to work with as a writer. However, if you start to dig deeper and do more research, you will discover a huge wealth of customs, traditions, beliefs, prejudices, styles, attitudes and other details which can not only make your story's setting pop, but also provide a treasure trove of ideas for story events which you might not think of if you didn't do the research.

This is again an advantage of basing your setting at least somewhat off a real place and/or time- it saves you the trouble of having to make up new ideas for story events or twists that might naturally spring from a real place. Of course, if you like making your settings from scratch, go for it, that can be a lot of fun too, but don't neglect the possibilities that come with real history and cultures.

EXAMPLES OF HOW CHARACTER, SETTING, AND PLOT INTERACT

As you have seen, these the three core parts of story – character, setting and plot - are a little more complicated than you were probably thinking when you first started reading this book. But, what's even more important to understand is how they interact, because while all stories will have Setting, Character, and Plot present, they will rarely be in equal amounts. Instead, one of the three will almost always be dominant in a story, while the other two will be less important, although usually not equal.

The truth is, you can do a story which focuses on any of the three, with the same story and characters, and get completely different results depending on which you choose to emphasize. For example, let's say we're doing a story about a young sushi chef rising to the top of her field like Hanna Tachibana.

In a Setting-based story, the emphasis will be about the world of being a sushi chef- the art itself, and the history and culture that goes with that art. It will be about why the apprentice system they use is so important, what fish is best for what, and the techniques they use in preparing those fish and turning them into beautiful dishes. The main character is the vehicle the author uses to take us into that world and experience it, and the plot is there to take that character from one situation to another where the chef can learn more about that amazing setting.

In a Plot-based story, the emphasis will be on the events that happen in the life of our young sushi chef as she tries to move up in her field. The focus will be on dramatic plot twists and surprise turns of events that will come at the character as she tries to make her dream happen. Her love interest will have a family gambling debt they have to help pay off. Her mentor will secretly have cancer, and is trying to impart the knowledge of the secret Ginzu Blade technique before they pass away, but pushing the main character so hard she threatens to quit. The rival sushi business across the street will cut off our hero's fish supply with dirty tricks, and force her to use inferior fish until that old fisherman she helped in chapter two brings her his catch. And so on, with the story going until the main character reaches their goals and/or the writer runs out of things to throw at them. The setting will be there to help provide a colorful background and story ideas, and the character aspect is there to give us some lively and interesting characters we want to see make it through a storm of troubles.

In a Character-based story, the emphasis will be on a main character filled with weaknesses, doubts, and insecurities who dreams of being a sushi chef. The focus will be on her growing and changing as she meets other people, learns new things, and experiences hardships. We will learn what it feels like to be a sushi chef, and how the main character is able to overcome her own personal flaws on her road to mastery. The dramatic energy of the story will come both inside the character and from her interactions with other characters with conflicting goals and needs, many of whom are trying to do similar things to the main character. Maybe a rival character is a 16th generation sushi chef trying to live up to their family legacy, or another is a foreigner from Nigeria who has come to Japan to learn and who now faces culture clashes and racial challenges. The setting will be there to influence and shape the main character's choices and way of moving through this world, while the plot will be there to keep things moving forward by giving the character challenges and surprises along the way.

So, as you can see, placing the emphasis on setting, plot, and character can each produce very different results, even with the same basic story idea. All three are always there, but the order in which they're emphasized can produce a big difference in what kind of story you tell and how the story is presented to the audience.

Which one you choose to emphasize should depend on a few factors.

1) Which type of story are you best at telling? Not everyone is good at telling all three types of stories. Some writers, especially beginning ones, are better at plot-based stories because they find it easier to focus on the dramatic events than spend time working through their characters' inner lives. However, some writers excel at creating or researching detailed worlds they want to explore, and others can immerse their readers in the lives of characters like nobody else.

2) Which type of story do you most enjoy telling? Do you love action-based stories built around events and cool twists? (Plot) Are you all about learning and sharing information with your audience? (Setting) Or do you want to take your readers on emotional journeys of change and personal discovery? (Character.)

3) Which type of story best suits this project? Do you have a goal with this project? What is it? If your goal is teaching about the evils of gambling culture, then probably you'd best to write a setting or character-based story. On the other hand, an adventure story about exploring distant stars probably fits better with a plot-based story or a setting-driven one.

4) How much space do you have to work with? What you're trying to accomplish with this project can make your options simpler. Character and setting-based stories tend to need more time because they're often trying to dig deep into people or the background behind something. Plot-based stories, on the other hand, are only limited by how complex the plot is and how many twists and turns you intend to throw in. You can tell a plot-based story in a 4-panel comic strip or short joke, whereas telling a character-based story in that short space would be much harder, and a setting-based story harder still! (Nothing is impossible, however.)

5) Which type of story does your intended audience want or expect? One of the most overlooked aspects of writing is that whenever possible you should write with an audience in mind. This means knowing your audience's expectations because if you don't give them what they want they won't be happy. For example, if you write a vampire romance as a plot-based action story, your audience will probably not be happy because you promised them character-driven romance, not action. As mentioned in #3, certain types of stories go best with certain genres, and you need to know which type your audience is expecting when you go into writing it.

Ranking your Choices.

One handy way to determine which of the three pillars is going to be important, and which isn't, is to rank the three of them in their order of importance from #1 (Strong) to #3 (Weak). None of them are likely to be equal, so make a clear decision from the start about which is going to be dominant and which isn't going to be important in your story.

Here's a list of options to help you in your decisions:

Setting

1. Strong: The story revolves around some aspect of the setting and is determined by it. Everything in that story is about teaching that aspect of the setting to the audience and all story comes from learning about that part of the setting the writer is trying to explore. The plot and character elements exist to serve the story's exploration of the setting.

2. Medium: The setting has a strong influence on the plot and events, with some parts of the setting influencing character decisions and story directions.

3. Weak: The setting is just there to provide color, flavor or background, and has no real effect on the plot or characters of the story.

Plot

1. Strong: The story is almost entirely driven by the plot. These events might be thrown at the character from outside forces, or the result of character actions, but they control what the character does and often how they do it. Setting will be there to support the plot and help generate story ideas, as well as add flavor to the story. Character will be there to provide a likeable antagonist and give the story a little more depth, as well as provide more material for plots.

2. Medium: The plot as a strong influence on the events which happen to the character or in how the setting is presented. The story will have a fair number of plot twists from outside forces or surprise results from character decisions.

3. Weak: The plot is just there to give a general sense of direction to the story and let the audience know it is moving in a direction of some kind. There may be some twists, but they will always be unexpected results from character or setting story elements.

Character

1. Strong: The story is rooted in the main character(s) and their personal needs and goals. The story will be about how they grow and change (or refuse to grow and change) as characters, and the major story points will come from their personal decisions and their interactions with other characters. Setting will influence who and how they interact with those people and grow, and plot will determine what challenges and surprises await them.

2. Medium: The characters are making clear choices from their needs and desires, and an important element of the story will be how the main character(s) change. However, the character's personal growth will be secondary to the setting or plot-based events, and only be there to influence things instead of drive them.

3. Weak: While there are characters, the characters have little to no change as the events of the story play out. They might influence the story with their decisions, but their influence and emotional states will mostly be there for color and flavor, and not significant to the plot or setting-based elements.

So, using the above tables, write down how you see your story being presented.

For example, a typical pulp adventure story like a James Bond movie, which puts emphasis on plot twists and character drama would look something like this:

1. Plot (Strong)
2. Character (Medium)
3. Setting (Weak)

On the other hand, a "kids collecting things" story like *Pokémon* tends to put emphasis on the background and setting over characters and would look like this:

1) Setting (Strong)
2) Character (Medium)

3) Plot (Weak)

And a Romantic Comedy story like *Bridesmaids* would put emphasis on the Characters and their interactions overall:

1) Character (Strong)
2) Plot (Medium)
3) Setting (Weak)

What will yours look like?

Note: You could ignore the 1-3 ranking system and just Rank them however you want, if you want your #2 and #3 to be equal for example, but there will almost always be a clear #1 because it will be such a strong influence on the way the story is told.

THE REASONABLE MAN

Irish Dramatist and thinker George Bernard Shaw once wrote the following in his 1903 book *Man and Superman*:

"The reasonable man adapts himself to the world; the unreasonable one persists in trying to adapt the world to himself. Therefore, all progress depends on the unreasonable man."

This quote sums up the relationship between setting and character nicely.

In character-driven stories, the story is normally built around a character who is trying to change the world around them to suit themselves- Shaw's "unreasonable man." That character may be on a heroic journey out to get fire and bring it back to their tribe, or they might be trying to solve a mystery and restore order, or maybe they're just trying to build a family, but by their very actions the setting is being changed and they are having an effect on it.

On the other hand, we have setting-driven stories- stories where the setting is dominant and the story is not about the character changing the setting, but the setting changing the character of the "reasonable man." This character may be entering a new world, or a society, or rejoining one, but these are stories of journeys inward, not outward, and stories of people finding their place in the world as it exists. Maybe the character is at the end of their heroic journey and just wants to come home, or perhaps they are tired of living apart and are seeking new connections, but if they want to be part of a setting, they must embrace it and conform themselves to it.

Naturally, some stories are about the conflict of these two positions- a character who wants to change the world deciding how much to let themselves be changed, for example. Perhaps they can reach some form of compromise, or perhaps the character will reject the world in the end, but that is still a story about the character's relationship with the setting. Generally, in stories which are driven by the character, the character will win, while in setting-driven stories, the setting will get the final laugh. Whether that's for good or ill is up to you, the writer, to decide.

AUDIENCE

"If you know your enemies and know yourself, you will not be imperiled in a hundred battles... if you do not know your enemies nor yourself, you will be imperiled in every single battle."

-Sun Tzu, the Art of War.

You might be wondering what the above quote has to do with writing, it's about war, right?

Wrong.

It has everything to do with writing, because at best a writer is only half of the storytelling relationship. The other half is the audience, and what happens in the heads of the audience while they experience the writer's story. Easily 50% of what successful writers do is find ways to connect with their audience in meaningful ways, and if you don't know your audience, like the ancient master of war said, you will find yourself constantly struggling to make your work connect.

Let's look at just a few ways in which a writer's understanding of their audience is important.

- A writer must know what language to use to reach their audience.
- A writer must know what their audience thinks and feels about a subject, especially if that subject is close to the thematic statement of the story.
- A writer can only use the archetypes in the heads of their audience. If the audience doesn't know them, then they must be explained in ways to let them understand.
- The writer must know what appeals to the audience and doesn't appeal.
- The writer must know how to make the audience feel the right emotions at the right times, or towards the right characters.
- The writer must know what the audience wants to get from the story.
- The writer must be able to market their work to the audience best suited to it.

- The writer must be able to shape their work to reach their target audience effectively.
- The writer must know what symbols are in the audience's heads and what those symbols mean to them.
- The audience must trust the writer to tell them a good tale.
- The writer must know what types of characters the audience expects and will resonate with.

So, as you can see, knowing your audience is a big part of being a writer, and if you don't plan for this and leave things to chance you're only increasing the odds that your work will neither reach your target audience nor be appreciated by it.

However, while this might seem pretty scary and intimidating to think about at first, there are a number of things you can do to make your life easier.

Know your Target Audience

The simplest thing for writers to do is know their target audience. This is simple because very often, the writer themselves is part of the target audience! We usually write the same type of things we enjoy reading, and so you only need to look in the mirror to know your target audience and what they like and don't like.

That said, just because you're part of the target audience doesn't mean that the majority of people who like this type of story like the same things you do about it. You might love a horror novel that you think is funny because you have a dark sense of humor, but the rest of the readership might actually love it because it's creepy and disturbing. If you write your darkly funny version of that type of story, then you will get people with a dark sense of humor, but might not get the ones who want to be scared because they're not there for the humor.

So, part of thinking about your audience is to think about how you may or may not be the typical audience member for that story. This is done through plain old research- reading the things you like with a close eye, talking to others, reading criticisms, and lurking on social media. You need to think deeply about what qualities connect you (and people like you) with the work, and know where you fit among the majority of its fans.

Another issue is tropes. Especially in genre fiction (mystery, sci-fi, horror, romance, fantasy, etc.) there are certain elements of the characters, setting, and plot which people who love that type of story both enjoy and expect. You need to know what those are, and how much your audience is willing to give you wiggle room on them and their presentation. Especially when you get into subgenres, it can become extremely specific what the audience wants to have happen and when. (Some Romance subgenres, for example, never go past the main characters holding hands, while other readers require characters to be sleeping with someone by the third chapter or they're out.) You also need to know what tropes the audience is sick of, or even hates, because while they might be things you yourself love, you're putting your audience appreciation at risk by including them unless you can do it well.

Again, tropes can only be learned by reading and research, but if this is your favorite genre that shouldn't be too much of a hardship as you know them by heart already.

But, what if you don't know your target audience? What if you want to branch into something new, or have been hired to write in a new genre?

Then it will come down to plain old research. Read what they read (preferably the classics or top reads of that genre). Read their comments. Know what they expect. And, think about what you would like or how you might react if you were them.

And that's also a big part of being a writer- putting yourself in your reader's shoes. Trying to empathize with them, and imagining what they'd feel and what would make them emotional, because that's going to be what makes them love your work.

CONNECTING AUDIENCE AND CHARACTERS

In the chapter on Plot, we covered Lee Floren's maxim that good stories are about, "An appealing character [that] strives against great odds to attain a worthwhile goal." And while every part of that sentence is important, none might be as important as the "appealing character" part. Audiences will follow appealing characters through anything, even poor writing, poor plots, and poor presentation. Appealing characters transcend authors, mediums, time, and even space- just look at the appeal of characters like Sherlock Holmes who is known throughout the world and so appealing that many treat him like a real historical figure.

But how do you make your characters so appealing that the audience will even trudge through the worst writing just to get a glimpse of them being their charming selves? Or, that you'll have fans waiting for every single new story that the character appears in like it was the birth of their own children?

The key to making them appealing comes down to one word-relatability.

If audiences can relate to a character, and feel a sense of sympathy towards that character, they will grow emotionally closer to them and form a bond with them. Or, the opposite, the less they can relate to a character, the more emotional distance they will keep from them, and the less they will like them. Using these two forces, like the positive and negative power of magnetism, lets authors push and pull the audience's emotions towards some characters and away from others.

For example, the simplest way to get any character and audience to connect is by showing they have (or don't have) a relationship with other people. As Blake Snyder pointed out in his book *Save the Cat!*, the moment we see a character acting as a member of the human family, we begin to relate to them and connect with them. You can see it in almost any film, television program, book, or comic when a character is first introduced- the lead character will almost always do something to help others, or show some positive connection with the human world around them. This tags them as a "good" person and the audience will automatically begin bonding with them and care about what happens to them on an emotional level. Sometimes it's small and subtle, like having photos of their family members, but it will always be there somewhere if the writer knows what they're doing.

To go into more detail, here are ten different ways that writers can bring audiences and characters closer together:

1. **Have them express relatable opinions** –The simplest way a character can make the audience like them is to have them say things which the audience would also say. This is because we like people who think the same things we do, as it makes us think our own ideas about the world are right, and we feel they are connected with us in some way. So, by having the characters express the feelings of the audience in words, it makes the audience want to like them, and want them to succeed.
2. **Give them sympathetic traits** – There are traits and characteristics that our society values like faithfulness, self-control, charity, having a decent work ethic, patience, kindness, and humility. These are the traits which make you a good person in the eyes of our culture, and we're taught to admire and respect the people who have those traits. It's no surprise then that if you give a character those traits, the audience will start to like and connect with them.
3. **Make them a good family member** – Being human means being part of a family, as all people (so far) have parents and people connected to them by blood. We judge others by how they treat the members of their family, and characters are no exception. If we see a character respecting their roles in

the family and being a good child, parent, grandparent, uncle, aunt or niece or nephew, then that draws us closer to them because we admire people who act like that.

4. **Make them a good citizen** – We are all a part of the society we grow up in, and when characters show that they're living up to the responsibilities that come with being part of their society it will make people admire them. For example, having characters respect and follow the law is a big part of showing they are a good person and member of their society. Also, having characters display the values of friendship, trust, generosity, caring, and respect for their elders will incline the audience to like them and consider them a good person. There is an old saying that we should judge people by how they treat those who they don't have to be nice to, so make your characters nice to people they don't need to be nice to and the audience will like them more for it.

5. **Make them a good friend** – Friends have been said to be the family you choose, and audiences respect those who treat their friends well. Whether it's their close friends, lovers, or even just acquaintances, we judge others by how they treat those closest to them, and whether they show the proper respect for the values of friendship- trust, honor, honesty, reliability, and occasionally putting your friends' interests ahead of your own.

6. **Have them take sympathetic actions** – Writing teacher Blake Snyder called this the "Save the Cat" effect, and told new screenwriters to have their lead characters do something nice (like saving a cat from a tree) in the introduction to make the audience instantly like them. While you don't have to do something so blatant, the more actions which a character takes that are what the audience would do (or want to do) in their situation, the more the audience comes to identify with them.

7. **Give them sympathetic reactions** – How a character reacts to a situation will be one of the biggest ways the audience decides if it likes them. If the character does what the audience would do, or similar things, then the audience will think that the character is a good person and should be supported. Also, if the character reacts in ways that express positive values (bravery, persistence, intelligence, thoughtfulness, etc.) the audience will like them because those are the values the audience generally agrees are worth supporting as well.

8. **Put them in sympathetic situations** – If you put characters into situations where they are the underdog, or where they are in a position of being the victim of outside forces, you automatically make the audience want them to

win, and thereby connect with them. Why? Because the audience also often feels put-upon and powerless, and they want to see other people in that situation win because it makes them feel like they can win too.

9. **Give them a sympathetic background** - If the character has a background that shows they have had a hard life, the audience naturally feels sorry for them. Why do you think there are so many orphans in fiction? Everyone knows what it's like to be alone and isolated, and everyone knows how they'd feel if they lost their parents, so an orphan represents their own worst fears come to life. Of course, you don't always have to go that far, just having bad experiences in a character's past can make the audience start to root for them- even if it's just having had bad breakup or a poor relationship with their parents. Also, it doesn't even have to be bad or tragic, just giving them a background like that of the audience members will often be enough to generate sympathy. (High school students often relate to other high school's students, for example, because of their similar life situations.)
10. **Make them entertaining** - If a character makes the audience laugh, or feel happy, then they will naturally want to connect with that character. This is why so many "best friend" characters are funny in some way- it makes the audience immediately like them and saves on character development. Audiences like people who make them feel good, and that includes characters as well. Funny = Instant connection.

Giving a character some of the above will make an audience like them; however, sometimes you don't want the audience to like a character, and in fact want them to actively dislike them. So, how do you do that? Simply put, you do the opposite of the above.

1. **Have them express disagreeable opinions** – If a character says something the audience can't agree with, then that will make the audience start to distance themselves from that character. As soon as the audience meets a character who doesn't share their values, they start to reject them and avoid connecting with them emotionally.
2. **Give them dislikeable traits** – Just as there are traits that the audience has been taught to admire in people, there are traits that we dislike, and we need go no farther than the Seven Deadly Sins to know what some of them are- pride, greed, lust, envy, gluttony, wrath, and laziness. In our society, people who show these traits are disliked, and looked down upon, and characters with these as dominant traits will be as well.

3. **Make them a bad family member** – A character who treats their family members badly is breaking one of the golden rules of society, and will instantly make the audience members dislike them.

4. **Make them a bad citizen** – Being a member of a society comes with "rights and responsibilities", and if a character only cares about their rights (what they can get from society) and not about their responsibilities (their duty to society) then the audience will often look down upon them. This includes taking advantage of others, not respecting society's rules or the law, and exploiting others and society's rules for their own personal gain.

5. **Make them a poor friend** – Since we value friendship so much as a society, we look down on people who treat their friends and those closest to them poorly. Those who abuse their friends and the trust of those closest to them are not seen as good people, and it can be a quick way to make the audience feel antipathy towards them.

6. **Have them take unsympathetic actions** – You could call this the "kick the cat" effect, and it simply means each action the character takes that goes against the values of the audience will make the audience dislike them. This is why many villain characters often will often do something bad right after they're first introduced- to establish them clearly as someone in the wrong. The more negative a thing the character does, the faster they'll be rejected by the audience and the more the audience will want to see them receive justice. Of course, many small disagreeable actions can also produce a disliked character as well.

7. **Show their lack of caring** – If the character doesn't react as the audience would or in ways the audience finds agreeable, then they will be further distanced from the audience. They will be interpreted as not being a good person because they show a lack of caring or empathy for their fellow man. This is especially true if they abuse others who have shown themselves to be good people, and do so without showing remorse for their actions.

8. **Show them abusing power** – If making a character the underdog generates sympathy, it's no surprise that making them powerful, and specifically someone who abuses their power, will make the audience dislike them. The audience knows what it's like to be powerless, so seeing someone abuse their power will make them dislike that person and sympathetic towards the victim of abuse.

9. **Give them an unsympathetic background** - This can work in two ways. One is to give them things the audience would want (money, power, a close family, admiration, etc.) and then have them waste it by abusing their good fortune. The other is to give them what would normally be a sympathetic background (poverty, abuse, illness), but then have them use that background as an excuse to be selfish and act in rough ways. If a character had a bad experience and then just whines about it and uses

it as an excuse to be lazy or cowardly, the audience will quickly go from being sympathetic to disliking the character.

10. Make them Boring - Audiences don't like boring characters. Boring characters feel like the audience's time is being wasted, and they start to get annoyed. Eventually, the audience will even come to hate them because they're taking story time away from other characters who are more interesting.

Through balancing these two approaches, you can control who the audience relates to in your story, using disagreeable actions to distance some characters while drawing the audience closer to others who share their worldviews. This is a fundamental technique of storytelling because it lets you play with the audience's emotions and how they approach scenes in a story.

For example, a very common technique in storytelling is to have characters do something agreeable or disagreeable while being introduced, with that being a marker to the audience to tell them that this person is "good" or "bad".

Let's take a scene where two chefs are introduced: Chef A and Chef B.

We want the audience to support Chef A, so he'll be introduced by helping a delivery man carry some heavy bags of rice into the restaurant while laughing and joking with him. Meanwhile, Chef B is busy yelling at his assistant chef for something small, and then comments that Chef A doesn't have to help, it's the delivery man's job, after all.

Right there, we've made the audience like Chef A, while Chef B is now seen as a jerk. If we continue to let those small patterns unfold in the following scenes of the story, then Chef A will progressively become someone the audience wants to spend time with and support. Meanwhile, Chef B will be more and more disliked and the audience will cheer at seeing him fail and get what he deserves for being such a nasty person. Layering on positive and sympathetic acts and negative and disagreeable acts over time is what will shade the characters in the audience's minds, and it can be much more effective to do this over time, as opposed to it having them do one big good or bad thing.

In fact, having them do something very good or bad when they're first introduced is a blunt technique that should only be used when really necessary, like what you will see in movies and television where they need to introduce a character fast because they don't have much time to work with. Watch for characters who act like big jerks the moment you see them, because those are the ones being set up so that they will get justice by the end of the scene. The writers want the audience to cheer when that character has something bad happen to them, so they have them do or say something bad right from the start and then let the scene play out with a bad end for that character. It also softens the audience's reaction to something bad happening to that person, so they consider it positive rather than negative and it doesn't affect their mood.

But what if you want to have a character start bad and have a change of heart? After all, some stories have characters that go on character journeys from being a bad or unlikeable person to a likeable one.

The answer to that is fairly simple- you introduce the character using their major bad traits to make them unlikeable, but then early on slip in a noteworthy good trait or action as well. This will make the audience pause and start to wonder about the character, as they have seen this person isn't all bad, and it will make them hold judgement until they have learned more about this person.

In fact, audiences like characters who are neither all good or bad, but who show traits from both sides because it makes them feel more lifelike and real. After all, no real person is entirely good or bad, and a few flaws often adds a lot to a character's personality and makes them more interesting. The key is balance, and making positive characters have more positive traits with just a few small flaws, and negative characters mostly negative, but giving them a few redeeming qualities. (That is, if you want the audience to be sympathetic towards them at all, because if you don't, then don't give them any real positive qualities as it lets the audience hate them without question.)

And, this leads to another way to make an audience connect with a character, one which isn't on the list because it's in a category all its own- are they acting out the audience's fantasies?

You see, your audience has fantasies, and if they see characters acting out their dreams then unsurprisingly they connect well with those characters. A simple example of this is a character winning the lottery, which the audience would also love to do, and then the audience wants to know how the character spends all that money because they know what they'd do if they won. On a more symbolic level, watching strong, cool, and capable characters do their thing is also a form of fantasy fulfillment for the audience. The whole American action movie genre is based on this- James Bond, Jason Bourne, John Wick, Deadpool, Indiana Jones, Captain Kirk, and any character played by Arnold Schwarzenegger (before he became Governor of California) are all characters who the audience wishes they were, and who are doing the cool things the audience wishes they could do.

Often these characters do things which are against the law, or even strongly negative (like killing others), but because they are surrogates for the audience (and the stories set things up so those murders are seemingly justified) the audience forgives them- just so long as they have a few good strong positive traits, it will all be fine. After all, sure they killed a whole boatload of people, but they did it for the love of their daughter, right? So, it's all okay! (Never mind that those people had wives, daughters and mothers too...)

By the way, this works in reverse too- if a character is acting out the audience's dreams, and another character appears which is going to interfere with those dreams, the audience will instantly hate that character with a vengeance. A good example of this is in romance stories, where a third character appears to try and steal away a member of the lead couple that the audience has invested so much time and emotion in. Any character which is a threat to the happiness of the main couple will provoke an extreme reaction because it puts the main couple's happiness (and the thus the audience's) in jeopardy. Bosses, school principals, and parents often fulfill this role too- we hate buzzkills, and want them to go away.

And finally, the last, simplest, and oddly the most powerful method of connecting characters and audiences- give them a name.

It really is that easy. Once you name a character, you make them a human being. Until you name them, they are a piece of the setting and an object the audience generally won't connect with. This is why an action hero can kill hundreds of enemy soldiers and the audience doesn't bat an eye- they're not people, they're obstacles and targets, so they don't count. However, the moment that action hero meets a named character, there's now drama and a sense of human interaction because we're looking at two people, not a person and an object for target practice.

Names are strangely powerful, as they have ideas that go with them in the minds of the audience. If the character is named John or Susan, and the audience members know people with those names, then there is an instant connection because those are the names of real people in their lives. Just like archetypes, names mean things to the audience members, and while the author can't control what the audience members feel about that name (it could be the name of their friend, or their hated bully from junior high) a name humanizes a character by making them a member of society. So, for example, in horror and romance stories the leads (and victims) will almost always have common names, it makes them more like real people to the audience. Also, supporting characters in many stories often have common names, because they're also the names of the supporting characters in the audience's own lives.

So, think about your audience, and choose your names wisely, they have more power than you think.

BUILD A RELATIONSHIP OF TRUST

The oft mentioned Greek Philosopher Aristotle once said that there are three forces that persuade the human heart- Logos (Logic), Pathos (Emotion), and Ethos (Trust) – and that of those three, Ethos was the most powerful of all. This isn't a big surprise because if you think about it, your whole world is built on a big pile of trust and belief in others. You trust people to stop at stoplights, you trust stores to accept money, you trust your friends to be loyal and keep your secrets, and so on. Without trust, human society falls apart and doesn't function.

Storytelling is no different.

The audience has many different choices of things to enjoy, especially in today's media-filled world, but they're choosing to spend their precious time with your story. They are trusting that you, the storyteller, will give them a good and entertaining story and not waste their time, and if you do waste their time they will leave and won't be back. (And won't give you more money, or ratings, or ad clicks, or good reviews, or whatever you crave.)

Also, a writer needs their audience to trust them because there will be times when you as a writer need to break the first commandment of writing ("Thou shalt not bore thy audience.") in order to set up the really interesting things that are yet to come. But, if the audience doesn't trust that you'll give them something they desire at the end of the long slog, they'll quit or stop reading before they get to it. They have to trust you, the writer, are doing what you do for a reason, and that it will all work out to their enjoyment in the end.

So, right from the start, a good writer must start to establish a solid relationship of trust with their audience, but how is this done?

Going back to Aristotle (was there anything this guy didn't know?), he said that there were three "C's" to Ethos that someone trying to win over an audience could use to build trust.

- Competence
- Character
- Charisma

Let's look at how each of these links up with fostering audience trust.

<u>Competence</u> – Right from the first word of a story, a writer is building a reader's trust in their competence- their skill as a storyteller. First, there are the basics, like not misspelling words, not making grammar mistakes, and using a wide variety of words to keep the story told in a lively way. Then there are the more

advanced things, like the ability to express ideas well, describe scenes and characters in the right level of detail, and make the reader always curious about what's going to happen next by using Dramatic Questions. All of these things, little and big, make a reader start to believe that a writer is a trustworthy entertainer who is going to give them something they want.

Character - As a storyteller builds trust with their skills at writing, they also make the audience trust them as a writer by how they act toward the reader. If they publish when they say they will publish, and are fair in their marketing, that will help to build credit with their readers. But, more than that, if they are clearly putting an effort towards telling the best story possible then that helps to make the audience believe they can trust this writer. Also, a writer of good character doesn't use cheap tricks to keep the story going but instead puts effort into providing the best quality product by playing fair with the audience, finishing their storylines, and knowing how and when to end the story. Audiences can feel when a writer isn't really into their work, and they will respond by walking away from substandard stories. However, if the audience comes to believe that this writer is committed to their craft, and someone they can trust, they will stick around.

Charisma – This is the writer's charm and ability to win over their readers with their style and writer's voice. Some writers have a natural storytelling manner that makes everything they write mesmerizing and makes the audience hang on every word- and this is charisma in action. However, even writers that don't have a natural gift in this area can develop their writer's charisma through dedication to their craft and developing their own "writer's voice" that makes their work unique. This is done through practice, practice, and practice, or to be more precise: writing, writing, and writing. The more you write, the more your writer's persona will be reflected in your work and make what you write unique. Audiences can sense this, and it makes them want to trust those writers to tell them something worth paying attention to.

Thus, all writers should be working to build a relationship of trust with their audience, and do so by using the Three C's. An audience which trusts a writer will forgive a lot of mistakes and keep coming back to the writer's work, because they know that this writer is one they can trust, which is something that sadly can't be said for every writer out there.

Be one of the good, trustworthy writers, and it will pay off in more ways than you can imagine, the least of which is a loyal fan base- which is what every writer wants, isn't it?

WHEN TO IGNORE YOUR AUDIENCE

One last thing that you should always remember is that the writer and audience are partners, not adversaries. The writer is making a deal with the audience, "I will write and entertain you, and you will in turn read it and give me support," and the audience is agreeing to it. Both sides want the story to be good, and both sides want the whole deal to succeed.

So, don't be afraid to work with your audience.

By this, I don't mean go on social media and ask them what should happen next. (Not a good plan, ever. It makes you look like you don't know what you're doing.) But don't be afraid of them either, and be ready to pay attention to how they feel about your stories and learn what works and what doesn't. Read some reviews (or have others read them for you and give you summaries, if you're thin skinned) and don't be afraid to lurk around or have exchanges with readers. The more you know them, and what they like about your work, the more you can try to find a happy middle ground between your goals and their tastes.

That said, whenever there is a conflict, put your own storytelling goals first.

Some writers get so caught up in writing for their audience they forget why they wrote in the first place, or let stories go off into different directions that vocal fans love, but that the majority of their audience might actually hate. There is also a temptation to spend a lot of time on social media when you should be writing, because it's so much easier and more fun than all that hard work.

But, if you don't do that hard work, those good times on social media will eventually come to an end.

Also, don't get too caught up in the constant social media wars and causes, they're a time suck and can make you afraid to write the story you want to tell. Don't let anyone tell you how to write your story, especially not people who are just trying to shape your work to support their social or political causes and agendas. Be willing to listen to honest criticism, but also be ready to separate fact from their personal opinions. Everyone is happy to tell writers what to write, because they're not the ones who have to do the demanding work of writing, but they get the benefits, so they have nothing to lose.

Tell your story, and learn when to ignore your audience, and when to listen.

There will always be haters, and you'll never make everyone love you or your work no matter how hard you try, so be true to yourself first and foremost.

WRITING STORIES - BRINGING IT ALL TOGETHER.

Now that we've looked at the five pillars, how can we use them to build a story?

Most of that is up to you. The five pillars are something for you to think about and use as you see fit.

While it is often best that stories start from a theme (and the Big Story Questions below are built around this), the truth is that writing is an art, so a writer can (and should) come at it from any angle or approach which works best for them. If the theme thing doesn't work for you, then don't worry about it, and if you're all about building settings and then populating them with characters and telling stories that way, then more power to you, have fun!

That said, to not at least spend some time thinking about each of the aspects of your story before you write it, especially if it's a long one, is probably a bad idea. Short stories you can whip off by the seat of your pants, and that works for a lot of people, but the longer and more complex the story is, the more time can be saved by doing some planning up front. Doing the work right at the start will very often mean less work during the editing and revision stage, and save both time and money. (And aren't those often the same thing if you're trying to make money writing?)

With that in mind, let's look at how you might approach building a story from each of the major angles.

(Visit my website at *robynpaterson.com* if you want an editable version of this chapter's questions and more!)

CHARACTER

Some writers like to think up an interesting character and create them first, which is perfectly reasonable. There are times when a character suddenly appears in your head in such vivid color that you can't not write stories about them, or when you see something that you think would be a great hook to build a character around. In cases such as these, the best approach is usually to develop the story from the character outward by asking a few simple questions.

1. Why is this person the way they are?
2. What kind of genre does the character belong in?
3. What kind of story is this character best suited for?
4. What kind of setting is this character going to fit in the best?
5. What audience would love this character? Why would they love them?
6. What themes does this character work best with? What would be the Thematic Statement that goes with those themes?
7. Who is the natural opponent for this character? What type of person? Why?
8. What supporting characters would bring out the best (or worst) in this character? Why?
9. What format best lets you explore this character?

Once you have these questions answered, then you can start to think about the Big Story Questions below.

PLOT

Sometimes you have a great idea for a plot, and you want to turn it into a real story. Maybe it is based on something from a book or movie you enjoyed, or an idea you saw in a video game, or perhaps it might be based on historical events or real-life experiences. Wherever you found it, you need to develop it before it can become a full story, and you can do this by answering a few simple questions:

1. Why do you like this plot so much? What about it is so interesting?
2. What kind of story is this plot best suited for? What genre and/or sub-genre?
3. What kind of characters does this story need to tell it? Which ones interest you the most? Which have the most dramatic potential?
4. What setting best suits this story? Why is that setting going to be the best place to put this plot?
5. What themes does this plot naturally work best with? What would be the Thematic Statement that goes with those themes?
6. Why would an audience enjoy this plot? What about it makes it so interesting? Or, how can you make it interesting?
7. What format best suits this plot?

Once you have these questions answered, then you can start to think about the Big Story Questions below.

SETTING

Perhaps you fell in love with a setting, and you want to make it into a story. Maybe it's a place you've visited or read about, maybe it's a place inspired by a piece of art, or even a song. Also, remember that settings aren't just geography, you can be inspired by architecture, fashion, arts, trades, mixed drinks, weapons, cultures, clubs, objects, sports or games. (To name just a few things.) Any part of the human world can inspire a story and anything shaped by human brains has a story behind it- one you can learn or dream up yourself. So, what can you do to develop that aspect of setting into a story? Start with these questions:

1. What is it about this setting (or part of a setting) that I find so fascinating?
2. If your story is about a part of a setting, what is the world which surrounds that aspect of the setting like? (The world of fishermen, or model kits, or goldfish breeding, etc.)
3. What type of stories can best be told about this setting? What genres does it work well with?

4. What kind of characters would naturally be connected with this setting? Which ones interest you the most? Which have the most dramatic potential?

5. What themes does this setting logically suggest? What would be the Thematic Statement that goes with those themes?

6. Why would an audience find this setting (or part of) as fascinating as you do? How can you make them feel that way?

7. What format best lets you explore this setting?

Once you have these questions answered, then you can start to think about the Big Story Questions below.

AUDIENCE

Maybe you have a target audience in mind, which isn't a bad idea. You may have heard this audience is looking for good stories, maybe you were hired to write for them, or perhaps you just feel a natural connection with that audience. This audience can be any age, race, sex, religion, demographic, gender, culture, or fanbase you want to divide people up into, and whatever it is, there will be people out there who can tell you how to market to them, because that's how money is made. So, with this in mind, let's start with a few questions:

1. Who is your audience and what defines them?

2. What kind of story or genre is your target audience most likely to enjoy? Why?

3. What kind of characters will connect best with your target audience? Which ones interest you the most? Which have the most dramatic potential?

4. What setting (or part of it) would your audience find most interesting? Why would they feel connected to it?

5. What themes will your target audience find interesting? What Thematic Statement are going to be most appealing to them?

6. What format of story does this audience like?

Once you have these questions answered, then you can start to think about the Big Story Questions below.

BIG STORY QUESTIONS

If you are a Pantser (someone who flies by the seat of their pants and makes the story up as they go along) then maybe these are just things for you to consider and help you as you write your way through the story. If, on the other hand, you are a Plotter (someone who plans everything out before they write), or someone who sits somewhere in between, then answering some or all of the questions listed below can help to guide you in preparing your story.

These are in what is probably the most logical order to do them in, but if you want to do them another way, feel free. It's your story, after all. The more questions you can answer, and in the more depth, the more you will understand the story you're going to tell.

Step One: Answer the following questions about your story.

1. What is the main idea of your story in one paragraph or less?
2. What is your story's genre?
3. What is your story's subgenre(s)?
4. Why are you the right person to write this story?
5. How long will this story be?
6. What is the format of this story? (Movie, Comic, TV Series, Web serial, Novel, Short Story, etc.)
7. How long do you think it will take you to write it?
8. What is your main motivation for writing this story? What do you hope to get from writing this story?

a. How will you maintain your motivation in writing this story if it's going to be a long one?

Step Two – Answer some or all of the following questions about your Audience

1. Who is my target audience?
2. Why are they my target audience?
3. Why will this story appeal to my target audience?
4. What about this story will appeal to my target audience?
5. How will this story affect my target audience?
6. What does my target audience know about my story's topic?

7. What does my target audience know about my story's theme?

8. What will my audience get from the story? And how will they get each of these things? *Skills? Perspective? (New perspective or Confirming perspective?) Information? Novelty? Emotion?*

Step Three: Answer the following questions about your story's Thematic Statement.

1. What is your story's Thematic Statement?
2. What supporting arguments can you present?
3. What parts of the story (plot) will support that Thematic Statement?
4. How will the characters reflect that Thematic Statement?
5. How will the setting and locations in the story reflect that Thematic Statement?

If you don't have a Thematic Statement, or don't know what yours is going to be, then pick a common theme, take a side, and make that your story's Thematic Statement. If you don't like it, or want to change it later because you came up with something better, then that'll be an option during revision. Alternately, if you're writing genre fiction you can just use the stock one(s) which come with that, but it's best if you take the time to think about what they are before you start.

If you don't want to have a Thematic Statement, then skip this phase and move on, you'll probably end up with one anyways thanks to your subconscious, but it may be a bit muddled. You can always find one in revision and then edit accordingly, but that is going to be a lot more work than figuring it out in the first place.

Step Four- Answer some or all of the following questions about your setting.

1. What is important for me to know about my setting? *People? Culture? Geography? Architecture? Technology? Other?*
2. Why choose this setting? Why is it the best setting for telling this story?
3. How does this setting reflect the Thematic Statement of the story?
4. How realistic is this setting?

If it is a real place, how much do I actually know about it?

If I don't know the setting, do I have easy access to resources about it?

5. What are the key locations of my setting, and what do they symbolize in the story and how do they represent the story themes and arguments?
6. How is the reality of the setting different from the one the audience knows?

7. What is the tone of the setting?
8. How does the setting reflect that tone?
9. What is the ranking of my story elements? Which is dominant? *Character? Plot? Setting?*

Step Five: Answer some or all of the following questions about each of your characters.

The Main Character

- Who is my main character?
- Why is that character the best character to use to tell this story?
- Is this character going to be Changing or Unchanging?
- If the character is Changing, how does their character arc reflect the Thematic Statement of the story.
- If the character is Unchanging, how does their personality and beliefs reflect the Thematic Statement of the story?
- What is the character's goal? Is that character's goal to... *Attain? Maintain? Lose?*
- What motivates this character?
- What positive personal traits does the character have, and how do they reflect the Thematic Statement of the story?
- What negative personal traits does the character have, and how do they reflect the Thematic Statement of the story?
- What physical traits (style of speech, body language, clothes, etc.) does the character have and how do they reflect the character and make them special?
- How in sync are my characters with the setting?
- How does the character's personal history reflect the Thematic Statement of the story?
- In what ways is this character going to be sympathetic to your target audience? How are they going to connect with this character?

The Main Opponent

- Who is my main opponent?
- Are they an Active or Passive Opponent?
- Why is that character the best character to oppose my main character?
- Is this character going to be Changing or Unchanging?
- If the character is Changing, how does their character arc reflect the Thematic Statement of the story in a negative way?

- If the character is Unchanging, how does their personality and beliefs reflect the Thematic Statement of the story in a negative way?
- What is the character's goal? Is that character's goal to...*Attain? Maintain? Lose?*
- What motivates this character?
- How does the character's goal put them in conflict with the main character?
- What positive personal traits does the character have, and how do they reflect the Thematic Statement of the story?
- What negative personal traits does the character have, and how do they reflect the Thematic Statement of the story?
- What physical traits (style of speech, body language, clothes, etc.) does the character have and how do they reflect the character?
- How does the character's personal history reflect the Thematic Statement of the story?
- In what ways is this character going to be un-sympathetic to your target audience? How is the audience going to be made to dislike the character?

Supporting Characters (answer these for each supporting character and opponent)

- Who is this character?
- What is the character's connection with the main character?
- What role (or roles) do they play in the story? *Ally? Motivator? Innocent? Resource? Catalyst? Comic Relief? Foil? Love Interest?*
- Why do they fill those roles? How do they fill those roles?
- Does this character have a goal? What is it?
- How does the character's goal motivated?
- Is that character's goal to... *Attain? Maintain? Lose?*
- How does the character's goal put them in support or opposition to the main character?
- What positive personal traits does the character have, and how do they reflect the Thematic Statement of the story?
- What negative personal traits does the character have, and how do they reflect the Thematic Statement of the story?
- What physical traits (style of speech, body language, clothes, etc.) does the character have and how do they reflect the character?
- How does the character's personal history reflect the Thematic Statement of the story?

- In what ways is this character going to be sympathetic or un-sympathetic to your target audience? How is the audience going to be made to like or dislike the character?

Background Characters (answer these for each character or group of characters in the story)

- Who are these characters?
- What role do they play in the story?
- How do these characters represent their group?
- How do these characters represent the ideas of the story?
- What do these characters want? (If anything?)
- Are they working in support or opposition to the main character?
- Are they working in support or opposition to the main opponent?
- What physical traits make them distinct?
- How will you make the audience feel sympathy for these characters or not feel sympathy for them?

Step Six: What is the plot of the story?

For each level of the story, figure out the Three-Act Structure, going from top (overall story) to bottom (chapter or scene). If you are using this for a Short Story, then you'll only need to fill out the Overall Story and the Scene list. If you're using it for a novel, then Overall Story, Chapter, and Scene would work fine. If you're using it for a Novel Series or Serial, then you'll need to fill out Overall Story, Story Arc (with each Novel being an arc in the series), Chapter, and finally each Scene.

Overall Story

<u>Act One: Setup and Problem</u>

- Who's involved?
- Where are they?
- What do they want? Why do they want it?
- What are their goals? (Attain, Maintain, or Lose)
- What actions are they taking to achieve that goal?
- What opposition will they face? (Active, Passive, Lack of Resources, Lack of Ability)

<u>Act Two: Interesting Events</u>

- What are the events which occur after they begin pursuing that goal?
- For each event, answer the following:
- What is the event? (Is it positive, neutral, or negative?)
- What is the reaction to the event?

Act Three: Apex and Resolution

- What is the climax of the story?
- How is the climax bigger and more significant than what came before?
- How will the climax reflect the Thematic Statement of the story?
- What is the wrap-up?
- How will this wrap-up reflect the Thematic Statement of the story?
- How will this wrap-up affect the characters and their relationships?
- Will the wrap-up leave anything open?

Story Arc (Fill out one of these for each Story Arc)

Act One: Setup and Problem

- Who's involved?
- Where are they?
- What do they want? Why do they want it?
- What are their goals? (Attain, Maintain, or Lose)
- What actions are they taking to achieve that goal?
- What opposition will they face? (Active, Passive, Lack of Resources, Lack of Ability)

Act Two: Interesting Events

- What are the events which occur after they begin pursuing that goal?
- For each event, answer the following:
- What is the event? (Is it positive, neutral, or negative?)
- What is the reaction to the event?

Act Three: Apex and Resolution

- What is the climax of the arc?
- How is the climax bigger and more significant than what came before?
- How will the climax reflect the Thematic Statement of the arc?
- What is the wrap-up?
- How will this wrap-up reflect the Thematic Statement of the arc?
- How will this wrap-up affect the characters and their relationships?
- Will the wrap-up leave anything open?

Chapter/Scene (Fill out one of these for each chapter or scene)

Act One: Setup and Problem

- Who's involved?
- Where are they?
- What do they want? Why do they want it?
- What are their goals? (Attain, Maintain, or Lose)
- What actions are they taking to achieve that goal?

- What opposition will they face? (Active, Passive, Lack of Resources, Lack of Ability)

Act Two: Interesting Events

- What are the events which occur after they begin pursuing that goal?
- For each event, answer the following:
- What is the event? (Is it positive, neutral, or negative?)
- What is the reaction to the event?

Act Three: Apex and Resolution

- What is the climax of the chapter or scene?
- How is the climax bigger and more significant than what came before?
- How will the climax reflect the Thematic Statement of the chapter or scene?
- What is the wrap-up?
- How will this wrap-up reflect the Thematic Statement of the chapter or scene?
- How will this wrap-up affect the characters and their relationships?
- Will the wrap-up leave anything open?

STORYTELLING WEAPONS AND TACTICS

This chapter is a collection of tricks, tips and methods you can use to make the job of writing your stories easier and improve the quality of your work. Think of them as a set of special writer's tools that don't really fit with the other fundamentals, but are important to know if you want to master your story writing craft. Naturally, all of them are optional, and can be used or not used as you see fit.

BRAINSTORMING IDEAS

There are many brainstorming techniques you can use to add some of your own originality to your story, however one of the best is *the Paradox Technique* (first suggested by UK Fantasy writer Michael Moorcock). It's a great technique that will work for almost any genre, and will really loosen up your creative juices.

Here's how it works.

Take out a piece of paper (or open up a word processing document) and set a timer for twenty minutes (or more, depends on you). Then, with your genre in mind, start to write down as many paradoxes (things that don't fit together) as you can in that time. The key here is to write down descriptive adjectives and adverbs and then pair them with nouns (people, places, things) and verbs (action words) that they don't normally go with.

So, let's say you were writing an office romance story, you might end up with some entries that look like this:

- Basement penthouse.
- Dry coffee pot.
- Page-less book.

- Useless computer.
- Tasty policeman.
- Ink Pencil.
- Blind glasses.
- Pickle wine.
- Wheel-less car.
- Singing plant.
- Hole-filled cups.
- And so on...

Don't stop before the time is up, and push the ideas as far as you can go, no matter how strange they may seem. The idea here is to tap into your subconscious and creative side. Then, when you've put down everything you can think of, look back at the list and the circle the ones which strike you as interesting or give you other ideas. Often a bunch of these seemingly strange ideas can be combined to produce scenes or story elements which make a different and unique story. While "pickle wine" might not factor into an office romance story well, if we combine "wheel-less car" and "tasty policeman" we might get an office worker who comes out to find her car's wheels have been stolen and ends up in a romance with the police officer who comes to investigate. Or maybe there's a practical joke war going on in the office, and some of the contradictions like "singing plants," "page-less books," and that weird "pickle wine" might start to make sense!

You can probably start to see now how useful and creative this technique can be, so try it yourself! Don't forget to include topics like people, jobs, machines, and other things that you'd find in the environment of your chosen genre story. And, if you don't know the environment, then add those to the list too! ("Dry swamp," "Bending skyscraper," "Sweet Street," etc.)

However, if you find the Paradox Technique doesn't work for you, another method is to create three columns on a sheet of paper. The first one is descriptive adjectives and adverbs, the second one is nouns, and the third one is verbs. Then take five to ten minutes to fill the three lists with as many words as you can that you associate with your chosen genre or story idea (if you have one already). After you've filled the columns out, go back and try combining the words you've listed in different ways, and see if any of those combinations spark ideas that you can develop into a story or parts of a story.

So, it might look something like this for a Space Opera story:

Adjectives	Nouns	Verbs
☐ Cold	☐ Space Station	☐ Fight
☐ Burning	☐ Starship	☐ Punch
☐ Steely	☐ Gun	☐ Shoot
☐ Sweet	☐ Tentacle	☐ Kick
☐ Rough	☐ Plastic	☐ Jump
☐ Wooden	☐ Goggles	☐ Toss
☐ Alien	☐ Flying Belt	☐ Embrace
		☐ Lose

Then you would start combining the words in different ways and seeing if any interesting combinations jumped out at you like "Alien Gun", "Steely Goggles", "Wooden Starship", or "Burning Flying Belt". From those we could get a story about a space ranger whose trademark is wearing steely mirror shade goggles and who finds a strange gun aboard an alien starship made of wood and must fight against raiders wearing flying belts who are after the alien ship. Or something like that! Maybe you see a different story in those words, and that's fine, the key is to just dump anything that comes to your head out onto the page and start playing with the lists to see what interesting combinations strike your fancy!

FINDING A CORE PREMISE

A Core Premise is the central idea of your story and a seed from which the rest of the story will grow. With it, you'll know the story you're trying to tell, and have a guiding star leading the way to the end!

To find your Core Premise, you're going to use a very basic technique that writers for movies have been using for a long time. In the movie business, writers often approach producers and directors with ideas for films, but they use a very simple structured version of their idea called a Logline to get maximum effect and make the producers interested. If they can use it to sell a movie to producers, you can use it to sell a story to yourself- so let's get started!

A great Core Premise needs to describe most of the following things:

1. One or two adjectives about the main character. (to give them personality)
2. The main character's role or job. (Don't use a name, just their role for now.)
3. Anything that's important to know about the setting or setup for the story.
4. What the main character's clear goal is.
5. One or two adjectives about the opposition. (to make them interesting)
6. The antagonist, opposition or challenge they face. (Also no names, use roles instead.)
7. A hint of what will happen if the protagonist loses, or the stakes involved. (to add drama)

These can be presented in any order, but usually go in the above order, and will produce one or two sentences that look like this:

A mousy college student (adjective, who) working in a used bookstore (setting) must find a mysterious book (goal) when her co-workers are possessed by evil spirits (adjective, opposition) that will escape the store at nightfall (stakes).

An overworked executive assistant (adjective, who) at a large corporation (setting) must choose between her work and her family (goal) when a long-time rival (adjective, opposition) threatens to steal a big project (stakes) during a family crisis.

A high school student (adjective, who) must find a way to tell her long-time crush her true feelings (adjective, challenge) before she moves to a new city and they lose touch forever (stakes).

It's actually pretty easy and fun once you get the hang of it!

Try using the ideas you brainstormed to come up with a Core Premise that follows the rules above. You don't need to use all the information you came up with, just the main ideas. Also, don't be afraid to try different versions of the premise with different details until you get one that you like.

Once you've turned at least one of your story ideas into a good-looking Core Premise, then you should ask yourself the following questions:

1. Does this story idea grab you and make you want to write it?
2. Is this story going to be one you think will interest your target audience?
3. Is this story going to make your readers feel something?

If a premise gets three solid answers of "yes!" then that's the story you need to write. If none of them get a "yes" for all three questions, then you need to go back and brainstorm some new ideas and turn those into premises that will work for you.

CHARACTER PROFILES

Some writers like to discover their characters as they write their stories, however there are also many writers who have found great success by creating detailed profiles of their characters before they start writing about them. As mentioned in the Character section, you should only detail the parts of characters you need, but what are the essentials for those people who like to have a clear idea before they begin their writing?

Let's go through what's useful and not so useful to know about each type of character.

Main Characters

The most important character in your story is your main character. They're the viewpoint from which the story is being told, and the reader's guide to the events which play out.

Main characters are also the trickiest part of the story to create, because they have to achieve the right balance of being unique while still being relatable to the audience. If the main character is too unique, the audience won't be able to connect and empathize with them because they're too different, but if the main character isn't at least a little unique they won't stand out in the minds of the audience.

The simplest solution to this is not to detail your main character too much, but instead make them special in a few important ways while leaving the rest unknown or vague so the audience's own imaginations can fill in the details and make them their own. This is one of the key skills of storytelling- giving the audience just enough to make a picture in their minds, but not filling in the details so that each person can make their own mental picture.

With this in mind, here's the top ten things to know about your story's main character:

1. **Basic biographical information**- age, sex, height, weight, hair color(s), job, family members, close friends, education, skills, work history, hobbies.

2. **What is the character's role in this story?** Main Character, Opponent, Ally, Motivator, Resource, Innocent, Catalyst, Comic Relief, Foil, Love Interest, etc. Pick one or more.

3. **What are they best at and what are they worst at?** Characters are often defined by their flaws more than their strengths, so make sure your character is bad at something for everything they're good at.

4. **What are the first things people notice about this character when they meet them?** Appearance, style of dress, style of grooming, manner of speech, body language, etc.

5. **What are two Paradoxes about them?** This is a fast way to make characters unique in the minds of readers- give them two things that seem to contradict each other in the minds of the reader. It also adds depth and interest to the character. For example, they're big and strong but very timid, they're a leader who is afraid of talking to people, they dress very conservatively but wear a brightly colored watch, or their personality changes when they're in a different environment. (Home/work/school.)

6. **What is going to make the audience like or dislike this character?** What about this character is going to make the audience connect with and care about the character? Or, on the other hand, what will make the audience dislike and reject the character? How will you as a writer make that connection with the audience?

7. **What is their overall life goal?** What, if anything, do they want to achieve in their life? What would be a perfect life for this character? What would they be willing to do to get it?

8. **What is their goal in this story?** A character's story goals generally come down to one of three things: attain, maintain, or lose. They want to get something they don't have. They want to keep something they've got. Or, they want to get rid of something they have. This isn't just physical things, it can be anything- objects, people, habits, money, knowledge, love, courage, safety, security, freedom, spirituality, and so on.

9. **What is their motivation in this story?** Why are they trying to achieve the goal in the story? What reasons are getting them off the couch and keeping them from running away? Why do they endure or try to escape? What keeps them from giving up and just being a victim?

10. **How does this character connect with the main theme of the story?** This is last, but one of the most important things to know- how does the main character reflect the theme of the story? Are they a weak person who learns to be strong? Are

they a strong person who inspires others to be strong? Are they are trying to change the world or restore the peace? How does the character represent the life lesson the writer wants the reader to know?

You should be able to fit the above on one or two pages of notes at most, anything more and the character is probably getting too detailed and may be harder for the audience to connect to. If you're an artist, feel free to sketch the character as well and think about their emotions and how they'd react to things. Other details will probably appear as you tell the character's story, and that's fine, just add them to the list as they come up.

Opponents

Creating a main opponent follows the same process as creating the main character. Use the above list of the top 10 things you need to know about the main character to build the main opponent as well. For Minor Opponents, you might not want to use the full list, but just focus on numbers 1,4,5,6,8,10. You really just need to know how they connect with theme, how they look, and what they're trying to do in the story.

Supporting Characters

Supporting characters are made much the same as minor antagonists, whether they're the mentors, friends, parents, lovers, co-workers, or any other kind of character that round out the main character's life. You just need to tell the audience their names, what they look like, give them a distinctive feature and something to do in the story, and you're good to go.

Background Characters

From a writer's perspective, it's generally best to limit these characters to archetypes and not to spend too much time on them. However, remember that they represent the world and setting the characters live in, so especially in visual mediums like comics and film you might want to give them some thought and make a few notes on how exactly they teach the audience about the setting and what aspects of the setting the background characters represent.

DRAMA AND THE RULE OF THREE

Humans love threes, especially in drama.

Three is the number where real action happens, because while two people can balance each other out, three is where the situation becomes unstable and unpredictable. All three might agree but more likely two will group together against one, and how that plays out is where the drama comes in.

Similarly, when structuring stories, a very common pattern is that characters will take three tries at any problem before they succeed. The first two times will always be a win and a loss, which creates drama and uncertainty around the now crucial third try, forcing the character to give it their all, and making the audience want to see how it all plays out. A good example of this can be seen in the American Three-Act Structure, which is the standard structure used by American writers. (See below)

In the American Three-Act Structure, the main character almost always faces their first big challenge during the first half of Act Two (usually at the story's 40% mark), and this challenge is one that the character will win. They try their best to solve the story's problem, they get good results, and everyone cheers for them as they can now see the finish line in sight. However, that's when the tables turn, as during the second half of Act Two (usually around the 60% mark), they will suddenly have their hopes crushed by the opposition. This failure will cause them to stumble and fall into the Dark Night of the Soul, where they are tempted to quit and just give it up. But, there is still enough of a spark of hope in them that it can all work out, so they pick themselves up, march into Act Three and around the 80% mark of the story they face their final challenge at the climax.

Used this way, the three tries become three smaller acts, where the main character first wins, then has the tables turned on them, and in the end must risk it all to win against a foe that has beaten them once and could do it again. It creates a strong dramatic cycle that has been proven to work in thousands of books and films, and which every audience member already knows subconsciously because they've seen it so many times. The audience knows the main character has the ability to win, but they also now know the enemy is stronger or equal, and so everything becomes about that big final moment.

Of course, you don't always have to use this win-fail-climax model that the American Three-Act Structure uses. For example, you could have a story where the main character succeeds in both of their first two attempts, but each try only gets them partway to their final goal, and then just before they make their third push something happens that puts their final win in question. Or, on the other hand, the main character might lose both of their first two tries, but from those losses they gain the knowledge they need to finally win in the end. Mixing it up keeps the formula from getting stale, and makes an audience used to the win-fail-climax model sit up and take notice as the story doesn't quite go as they expected.

Also, you could have only two attempts, or four or more tries instead of three, breaking the mold even further. However, be careful when doing this as odd numbers are natural tie breakers that everyone understands intuitively, so when you make the numbers even it doesn't feel as dramatic. Also, a character taking two tries at solving their problems might feel too short, and a character making four or more major attempts might run too long. Three tries fits nicely into the three-act structure of stories, and paces well. (Even if the first two tries are crammed into Act 2.)

Finally, remember that these are major attempts the character makes to solve their problems and goals, and the character likely makes a lot of smaller attempts in between as they work up to each of the major tries. These smaller attempts can best be understood as what is commonly called the Try/Fail cycle...

THE TRY/BUT CYCLE

There is a common bit of writerly wisdom floating around the Internet that good stories are built on what is called the "Try/Fail" cycle. Where characters take actions, fail in those actions, regroup to try again, and eventually reach their goals through endless tries and experimentation. This idea isn't new, as you can even see it in Syd Field's manual for screenwriters *Screenplay*, which was published in 1979 and describes the Scene-Sequel pattern of writing scenes. In this pattern, a character tries to accomplish part of their greater goals, fails, and then spends the next (Sequel) scene trying to find their new direction before become active again and trying something else.

Neither of these approaches is completely wrong, but neither of them is exactly right either.

The problem is that any scene in a story where a character is pursuing goals actually has five possible endings: success, failure, partial success, partial failure, or unexpected results. And, a good story is going to see a mixture of all five of these types of endings used in different combinations and different ways to produce various effects. Failure creates tension and drama, and brings the character's victory into question while also exploring and eliminating possible answers. Success brings hope, and keeps the audience from getting too pessimistic. Partial failures/successes keep the story moving while making the character work hard to achieve their goals. Unexpected results introduce surprise twists and turns that keep the audience guessing and reading. All of these are needed tools of drama, and trying to reduce the name to something as simple as the "Try/Fail Cycle" gives writers the wrong idea about how it all works.

Nevertheless, thinking of stories as a series of cause and effect actions and results is actually a useful tool for story planning and plotting. The key difference, however, is that most scenes in a story don't end with outright success or failure, but almost always end in partial success/failure, or unexpected (but reasonable) plot turns. So, rather than think of it as a Try/Fail Cycle, the better way to approach it is to think of it as a Try/But Cycle- the character succeeds/fails, BUT not completely or with unexpected side effects.

Examples:

- Sue tries to buy a cat, but the store only has a strange kitten missing an eye.
- Ken tries to please his angry wife, but just when she's calming down his co-worker texts him with a flirty message and his wife sees it.
- Thala breaks into the bank to steal the gold, but once inside the security codes don't work.

Using this approach, while mixing in some actual real successes and failures at key dramatic points, keeps the story flowing forward. The key is that the character is progressing towards their goals, but it's often "two steps forward and one step back," and they need to keep rethinking how they're going to achieve their short and long term story goals.

Two of the pioneers of this technique are Trey Parker and Matt Stone, creators of the TV show *South Park*, who use a refined version of this when getting their shows famously to air within a week of starting production. They need to be able to plan stories fast and efficiently, and thus they use their version of the Try/But cycle to quickly map out how the story will go each week.

Here's how it works for them- everything comes down to four key words, which are **but**, **and so**, and **meanwhile**. Using these four, they string together stories into logical sequences of events like this:

- Bob drove to the store to buy milk.
- **But**, there was a robbery in progress.
- **And so**, Bob called the police.
- **But**, the robber hijacked Bob's car and made him drive at gunpoint.
- **And so**, Bob found himself in a police chase.
- **But**, instead of being scared, Bob actually started to enjoy himself.
- **And so**, he used his knowledge of the city to evade the police and escape.
- **But**, the robber was going to kill Bob as a witness.
- **Meanwhile**, Bob's wife Anne saw Bob on the news and rushed to the police station.
- **But**, the police ignored Anne.

- **And so**, she decided to take matters into her own hands and find Bob.
- **Meanwhile**, Bob told the robber that he wants to join him and become the man's get-away driver.
- **But**, the robber was still suspicious and told Bob to drive to an abandoned warehouse.
- **And so....**

The story can go on from there as long as you want, in a clear cycle of actions, results of different kinds, and multiple lines of characters taking action at the same time (represented by the "meanwhile"). Sometimes the characters will succeed, sometimes they'll fail, but mostly they'll move from one problem to another, which will keep the plot hopping. Instead of a story of failure, it's a story of action and reaction, with twists and turns designed to keep the characters and audience guessing.

You can use this method for planning novels, chapters, serials, or any kind of story, but it works best with active action-driven stories where the lead characters are driving the story through their actions. Each sentence should start with the name of the character taking the action, and an active verb which describes the action they're taking. Avoid passive verbs like "is" and "has" which don't really describe anything the character is doing or give a sense of what's happening in that scene. (ie not "He is on the corner." but "He waits on the corner.")

THE GUN, THE CAKE AND THE WAVE

The Gun

One of the most crucial skills any storyteller can have is the skill of being able to set up and pay off story elements. This is pretty natural, when you think about it, because stories themselves are about people doing things (setup) and then getting results (payoff). So, it's no surprise then that being able to set up story elements and then pay them off later is at the very heart of storytelling.

We could use any number of metaphors to describe this relationship- planting and harvesting, cause and effect, Laurel and Hardy- but the most famous version comes from Russian playwright Anton Chekov who said, "If you place a gun on the mantle in the first act, you need to use it by the third." This famous phrase is now referred to simply as "Chekov's Gun" and what he meant by that consists of two things:

1. You should introduce nothing of significance in a story without using it as part of the story.
2. Everything of significance in a story should have a purpose and reason for being there.

So, to put it another way, everything in a story should have a reason for being there, and if you include something in a story you need to be using it in some way. Stories, after all, are about efficiency, you can't simulate a whole world in a story, it isn't possible even in film, much less text, and you don't want to waste the reader's time (lest they get bored), so you can and should only mention things that are relevant to the story being told.

In the same way, once you introduce something, it should be useful to the story being told in some way. It doesn't matter if it's there to reveal setting or character, or is there to explain or set up plot, but nothing you include in a story should be meaningless. And this goes double for things that you the author call attention to, because the audience is subconsciously looking for those clues, and if they don't see them paid off or explained in some way, they're going to get annoyed.

So, how can you set these things up in your stories?

One useful way is to think of things that happen in a story as being chains of cause and effect- so nothing that happens (an effect) should occur without a reason (cause) which is either presented, explained, or hinted at somewhere in the story itself. There should be no random events or acts of god which cannot be explained logically, and there should be no situations where the characters just do things for no reason. Those only result in bad storytelling.

And the more major the effect, the more setup and detail is often needed by the cause. If you want the audience to have a major reaction to something, you can't just have an event happen, you need to slowly or clearly set it up. Audiences react to major events precisely because they understand the reasons, the stakes, and the possible consequences of those events- and all of this requires the writer to explain them before they occur. (Or occasionally after, in some dramatic structures.)

Also, big events are often made up of many smaller events, just like a chain reaction which causes bigger and bigger things to happen as it goes along. And one easy way to think about these types of reactions in stories is to use not only cause and effect, but also to make sure each result does actually have an effect of some kind-often the unintended sort.

Events happen because other events happened, and once you start a chain it can continue on as long as you want and branch into multiple directions depending on who is affected and why. The writer's job, once you get the hang of this, isn't to think of more things that could happen, but to try to reduce the number of things that could happen to just what you want to have happen. Also, remember the rules about being consistent in your presentation and playing fair with your audience.

The Cake

Speaking of audiences, one of the other great skills a storyteller must have is the ability to pace the story out so that it reaches the climax at the right time. And, to do this, you must always follow one of the most simple rules of storytelling- don't give the audience what they want.

You might find this confusing, since after all, the goal of a storyteller is to entertain an audience and keep them happy, right?

It is, but it comes down to what a very smart friend of mine refers to as the "Chocolate Cake Paradox."

The Chocolate Cake Paradox goes like this: People love chocolate cake, and if you give them chocolate cake they will eat as much as they can. However, if you let them eat too much chocolate cake, because it's so sweet they will quickly get sick of it and won't want chocolate cake anymore.

Stories are like this too. If you want the audience to stay, you can't give them too much action, or too many major events in a row, or they will get sick of it and become bored. They might be there for the really cool scenes, but those scenes are only really cool because you set them up, and because they're saved for the best spots in the story. So, you have to pace the story out so that the biggest (and sweetest) parts are saved for near the end, and make sure that things start low and build rather than turning it up to eleven at the introduction and having nowhere to go.

This doesn't mean you can't have a big action or event opening, but you need to follow it with something slower and more focused on character or story development, and then work your way back up the major events. It's all about rhythm- like riding a wave.

The Wave

The same friend who posited the chocolate cake theory also once commented that many stories run like Sine Waves. If you haven't seen them, a Sine Wave is a mathematical curve which describes a smooth up and down oscillation that doesn't end. The line goes up and down, up and down, like a series of waves that can be tightly packed or far apart, depending on what they're representing.

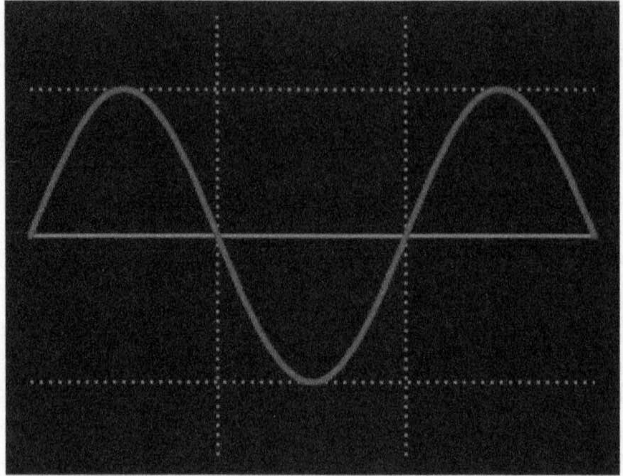

While stories should always be rising in their dramatic and/or tension levels, it isn't a direct line like so many charts often present it as. Instead, it's actually a series of waves, and many small rising and falling motions that while generally moving up aren't doing it constantly but taking breaks to let the audience breath. Quick dialogue is broken up by slower exposition. Exposition heavy scenes are paired with dramatic scenes. Characters advance, and characters stumble. Everything moves forward, and everything rises, but it does so in a smooth rhythm. Not too fast, and not too slow, but at just the right pace for what the writer is trying to accomplish.

That is the art of storytelling- everything there at just the right place, pace and time.

The gun, the cake and the wave.

GETTING PUBLISHED

When it comes to getting your work published, there's good news and bad news.

The good news is that you have decided to put your work out into the world at a time of transition, when the old models of top-down publishing are falling away and there has never been more opportunity to get your work out there for people to see. Your audience is now potentially global, which means your work can also be seen and enjoyed by roughly 3.2 billion people. Also, there are now more markets than ever, with various websites in different languages ready to promote work they think their audience wants to see, and even share the profits with creators.

The bad news is that any of those 3.2 billion people can also publish just like you, and quite a few of them have, and so it's created a flooded market where even the best work is hard to find in a sea of really bad stuff. At the same time, the big publishers are slowly dying, and the whole ecosystem for promoting, selling and marketing books in English is slowly falling apart.

Authors have never had it worse, but even in the bad times, there are always opportunities. So, let's look at the available markets for getting your work out there.

The Ebook Market

At the moment, roughly 40% of Amazon's book sales are of ebooks, and so naturally any writer should consider self-publishing their work as ebooks as an option. There is a huge wealth of wisdom regarding this subject online, and David Gaughran and Chris Fox are two names you should look up if you want to enter the ebook market. Both of them have written books to walk you through the process, and you can find more information about self-publishing on forums like kBoards and Absolutewrite.com, and the Creative Penn podcast.

However, the ebook market is not a place for the faint of heart. Yes, it's easy to get in, but because of that the competition is massive and writers need to also be skilled marketers if they want to get any success. If you're a new and unknown writer, don't expect any attention, feedback, or sales unless you get very lucky or have an amazing product with an amazing cover (sad to say, it seems like most ebook sales are due to their covers, not their content). This is a little easier if you're publishing ebook versions of graphic novels, since there's less of them, but even then it will be a hard battle to get noticed.

If you do decide to brave the vast ebook seas in search of treasure, here are a few tips:

- Get the best cover you can afford.
- Get the best editing you can afford.
- Pick a genre and build your reputation in it, don't jump around between genres.
- Write a series, not stand-alone books.
- Write fast, publish often.
- Research the market, it literally changes every few months.
- Expect to write at least three books before you get any real audience.
- View every book you write as a lottery ticket- it might yield nothing, or it might be a hit. You never know until you put it out there.

Webfiction

Leaving the paid markets, you might want to try writing webfiction as a way to practice your writing craft. Big sites like Wattpad, Fictionpress, and Fictionhub offer the potential of huge audiences for original work, and they also let you network with other writers and fans to build up your own personal reputations. Some of these sites will also do profit sharing on the more popular stories, sharing ad revenue with the authors, and will help to promote the works they see as worthy. They also don't usually lock you in (read contracts carefully), so once your story is done you can turn around and also publish it as an ebook (see below) and find new audiences and sources of revenue.

On the downside, as usual it's hard to get noticed on these sites unless you're really good, and each hosting site has its own audiences. Wattpad, for example, started out as a fanfiction site, and as a result has a huge audience of female teen readers, and a much smaller one of males and non-teen readers. This is great if they're your target audience, but if they're not your target audience you might find trying to get an audience for your story there more difficult. Also, there is the issue of style- a lot of popular webfiction seems to be more of the "Light Novel" style, which is dialog driven and uses narration sparingly. So, if that suits your style, you're set, but if it doesn't then you might find it harder to build an audience. Finally, there isn't much money in webfiction unless you illustrate your works and can then turn those illustrations into merchandise.

Conventional Publishing

Finally, if you want to publish fiction and your dream is to have a publisher do the marketing while you just write and bask in book tours, there's something you should know- that kind of author/publisher relationship doesn't exist anymore. Even if you sign with a big publisher, at best you'll get a US$5000 advance (down from US$20,000 over two decades ago) and still be expected to do your own marketing and all the work you'd have to do if you self-published. In return, you'll get around 7% of the profit of each book sold in the almost extinct bookstore market, as opposed to the up to 70% you get from self-publishing.

All this, after potentially years of waiting to hear whether your book was accepted by the big publishers, when it could have been out there making you money and building your career as a self-published book.

However, the big publishers aren't the only ones in the game anymore. There are now a number of small-press publishers who offer good terms, help with marketing, and even help with editing and covers. So, if you want to see your work in bookstores, but don't want to give up all your rights to a big publisher, do some research into small-press publishers and see if you can find one which might work for you.

FINAL THOUGHTS

Earlier in this book, I quoted Tennyson's famous poetic lines "To strive, to seek, to find, and not to yield," as an example of something that has to be used at the right place and time.

Well, this is that right place and time.

After reading this book, you now have the basic fundamental knowledge you need to write stories of all kinds, from audio dramas to comic books to feature films. All stories run on the same basic ideas that we've been developing as a species since the beginning of time.

And now- it's your turn.

Using this information, you need to strive to write the work that brings your unique vision to the world. You need to keep seeking your own personal Shakespeare Code that will let you produce the best work you can in the shortest time. You need to keep writing to find out what works best for you and keep learning about your craft by sharing knowledge with other writers. And finally, you need to never yield to that inner voice or critic which says you're not good enough and that you'll never be a "real" writer.

There are no "real" writers, there are only people who find their audience and people who don't. The way they find that audience, the size of that audience, and the people who make up that audience depends on each writer and their own goals and desires.

In the three-act story structure, there is a character (you), an action (being a writer), and a result.

The first two parts are already in place.

Now the results are up to you!

Good luck, and never stop telling stories!

Robyn A. Paterson

CPSIA information can be obtained
at www.ICGtesting.com
Printed in the USA
LVHW091258031221
705187LV00017B/172